1986 Gardener's Almanac
SEASONAL
Celebrations

Jeff Cox

Illustrated by Barbara Field

 Rodale Press, Emmaus, Pennsylvania

For Dad.

Book design by Linda Jacopetti
Art direction by Karen A. Schell
Edited by Anne M. Halpin

Library of Congress Cataloging in Publication Data
Cox, Jeff.
    1986 gardener's almanac.

    1. Gardening. 2. Seasons. 3. Almanacs,
American. I. Title.
SB450.965.C68   1985   635   85-2057
ISBN 0–87857–535–9   paperback

2   4   6   8   10   9   7   5   3   1   paperback

Contents

Acknowledgments

Special thanks to Derrick H. Pitts, Chief
Observational Astronomer at the Franklin Institute
Science Museum in Philadelphia, and to Richard
Schmidt at the U.S. Naval Observatory in Washington,
D.C., who supplied the astronomical information for
this book.

Appreciation is also extended to the publishers who
granted reprint permission for the poetry quoted in
this book:

"Berries" (page 84), by Walter de la Mare. Reprinted by
permission of The Literary Trustees of Walter de la Mare
and The Society of Authors as their representative.

"Envoy" (page 125), by Ernest Dowson, from *Modern American Poetry, Modern British Poetry*. Reprinted by permission
of Harcourt, Brace, Jovanovich, Inc., New York.

"Nothing Gold Can Stay" (page 51) and "The Bear" (page
111), by Robert Frost. From *The Poetry of Robert Frost*,
edited by Edward Connery Lathem. Copyright 1923, 1928,
1969 by Holt, Rinehart and Winston. Copyright 1951,
1956 by Robert Frost. Reprinted by permission of Holt,
Rinehart and Winston, publishers.

"One Hard Look" (page 77), by Robert Graves. Reprinted
by permission of Curtis Brown, Ltd. Copyright 1958, 1961
by Co-Publications Roturman S.A.

"Good and Bad" (page 64), by James Stephens. Reprinted
with permission of Macmillan Publishing Company from
Collected Poems, by James Stephens. Copyright 1912
by Macmillan Publishing Company, renewed 1940 by
James Stephens.

"Winter Time" (page 20) and "Summer Sun" (page 89),
from *A Child's Garden of Verses*; "Requiem" (page 139), from
Underwoods, by Robert Louis Stevenson. Reprinted courtesy of Charles Scribner's Sons.

Introduction

Seasonal celebrations tick off the times that measure our lives. In celebrating the passage of time, we welcome the grand cycle — from birth to death — and our tour through it.

We're alive! And lucky to be so. We've been provided with a body to work with, a mind to think with, and a spirit to set our course. Without open acceptance of the grand cycle, life can become isolated, routine, fearful. Celebrations change that. They charge life with mystery, magic, and meaning. They give us the opportunity to appreciate the milestones of our long journey.

The Grand Cycle and the Little Cycles

There's a connection between the grand cycle and the seasons. The year is born in spring, flowers in summer, fruits in autumn, and then dies away. Within the year, countless creatures live their tiny allotments of time. And yet, any life is a whole life, whether it lasts a minute or a century. The seasons correspond to youth, young adulthood, middle age, and old age. By watching their progression, we can see where we've been, where we are, and perhaps something of where we're going. Celebrating the seasons brings these correspondences and meanings to life. The result: new perspectives and a heightened enjoyment of living.

Cycles in the Garden

The garden is where we touch the earth. Both the grand and the little cycles go round there. By stepping into the gardening process, the gardener meshes gears with these cycles. Each season has its own processes: planting in the time of infancy; weeding, watering and protection in youth; full flowering in adulthood; and the payoff of harvest as the plants bear and ripen fruit. In senescence, the plants' old age, they are torn out and placed in the compost pile. There they will decay into rich humus and become the bed for next year's seeds. Compost is thus the source and the destiny of the garden's life. Since analogous processes occur within each person, gardening is a fine way to heed Socrates' injunction to "know thyself."

Changes in the garden are almost imperceptible, like the hands of a clock that don't seem to move if you stare at them. But the garden is inexorably changing in ways so subtle they are seen only with hindsight. For example, two weeks ago the tulips and scilla in my rock garden gave it a red and blue theme. Now it's yellow and lilac, as doronicum and bugle weed replace the fading bulbs. I didn't even notice when the first color scheme disappeared.

The seasons also move imperceptibly but constantly. Frosts, heat, wind, and moisture have their days and then vanish. The force that drives the seasons drives the changes in the garden. The great wheel turns the small wheel, and people turn with them both. Who hasn't felt elated and hopeful on a spring day? Warm and grateful in summer sunshine? Satisfied and wealthy at harvest time? Melancholy as summer dies before the frosts? Hunkered-down and holding on during the fierce part of winter? Anxious and expectant in the days before spring begins?

2

A Natural Calendar

If nature, the seasons, and our gardens have so much to tell us about ourselves, perhaps we'd better listen more closely. But how? In our culture, we mark off the year with months — meaningless names for periods that correspond with neither the moon's phases nor the solar cycle.

The names of the months are mere conventions: June is named after an ancient goddess; July and August recognize Roman emperors. Although Oct-, Nov-, and Dec- are the Latin prefixes for 8, 9, and 10, they are affixed to our 10th, 11th, and 12th months. The names of the months have no real relation to the seasons or to nature.

The moon recycles herself every 29½ days — yet only February reflects that, and then for only one out of every four years. The length of each day doesn't divide evenly into either the moon or sun cycle, and so our traditional calendar has been jerrybuilt in order to have months of relatively similar lengths and a year that needs only occasional correcting. Because of this, our calendar has lost its original connection with the seasons. But wouldn't it be nice if our calendar did mark the moon's phases, so that we could recognize them as they passed? And wouldn't it be nice if, instead of honoring goddesses and emperors, calendrical periods marked the procession of natural events and additionally reminded us of something to cheer about?

What if we forget about months and weeks? If we drop our preconceptions about how the year is arranged for the convenience of our culture? What we're left with is, first of all, the natural day, one spin of the globe, which is 23 hours plus 56 minutes and 44 seconds long. We could divide our year into periods that follow the moon: It waxes and wanes in just over 29 days, marked by the full and new moon points that recur about every 14 days. We also have the cardinal points of the solar year: the spring and fall equinoxes and the summer and winter solstices, which are natural demarcations. And, through it all, we have a steady progression of the seasons.

The 24 Chinese Periods

The Chinese long ago integrated these natural phenomena into one lunar-solar calendar, which divides the year into 24 periods. These begin on either a full or new moon, or on the equinoxes and solstices. The periods average about two weeks long, although some are longer and some shorter as the equinoxes and solstices interpose themselves into the regularity of the moon's cycle.

Each of these 24 periods is named for a natural feature of its time of year. The names are very ancient and correspond to the climate around Beijing (formerly Peking), which is very similar to much of temperate North America.

The names of these periods are poetry. You'll notice that The Period of Beginning of Autumn falls in the first half of August, in the heat of the Dog Days. I've watched for some signal that summer is not invincible during those weeks and, sure enough, there's a shade less intensity to the sun. The first few walnut leaves fall into our driveway. The fields begin to hum and shrill in a chorus that will reach a crescendo with the katydids in September. Summer hangs ripely. And it is just then, when the summer has spent its vital energy and is cresting, that the new note of autumn is sounded. It may be just a hint, but it's there. The Chinese are right on target. These periods form the basis for this book.

The 24 Seasonal Celebrations

The Chinese periods are very classical and formal. But there are other things going on in those periods that are peculiarly American in interpretation, things we might not always think of celebrating. Like "Mud Time." Now that we're grown up, spring mud time is just a difficult annoyance. But remember when mud was the universal goop out of which kids could fashion pies, grenades, logs, and so much more? With a light attitude and a heart ready for a good party, we'll find a cause for celebration in all 24 lunar-solar periods.

A Lunar-Solar Calendar

This almanac contains a calendar that's both lunar and solar. It's lunar because the periods are marked off by the dates of the new and full moons and solar because the equinoxes and solstices are given periods of their own at the cardinal points of the year. The calendar is based on a homemade version my family has kept for years, which was itself inspired by a Chinese calendar published by the New Alchemists about ten years ago.

I believe that if you follow the natural year with this almanac, you'll get a better feel for the rhythms of the moon and sun, for perceptible changes in the seasons, and for the mythic quality of life's cycles of growth and decay. Watch for the correspondences between the Chinese periods and your local environment. During The Period of Awakening of Creatures, see if you can detect any stirrings from under winter's cold litter. You'll find that the periods are usually very accurately named and reveal subtleties in nature you may not have noticed before.

What we're celebrating is life. Its recurrence each year cheers us; our participation in it should thrill us.

The seasonal celebrations in this almanac are suggestions for the kinds of things we usually ignore but should be celebrating, or at least noticing. For instance, sometime in the middle of August the birds start to gather, making first preparations for the later migrations south. I imagine the user of this book might take the kids on a picnic and mention that the birds are gathering now.

Can you see them? Are there flocks now, where before there were only nesting pairs? What huge and unseen process is urging this phenomenon on? Do we also get the urge for going?

To be aware of the birds and their movements is to be engaged in nature in some way that affects us deeply. These meanings will never die, because they occur again next year, as fresh as youth each time they return.

The ideas in this almanac are ones that have inspired me and many others to celebration. May they inspire you, too! After all, celebration really needs no reason. Somewhere in our hearts, in a quiet way, there should be a constant outpouring of gratitude and wonder that we are here at all.

The Natural New Year

'Long about September, nature's green cities begin to dry out and blow away. Through the months that follow, the year ages and the days grow colder. It declines toward death on the darkest day of the year, December 21. Now the light has withdrawn and ice seems to be the victor. The world of summer lies in ruins, frozen and dead.

8   The very moment of death, however, is the moment of rebirth! From December 21 on, every day grows a little longer. The seed catalogs arrive. It's a new beginning. Under the snows, locked in the frozen soil, the seeds and roots are set to grow. Though they'll sleep until spring, a spark is kindled at the solstice in each of life's little reservoirs.

That's the mystery—that the darkest hour is just before dawn, that the moment of the old year's passing signals the start of the new.

The light may be dim and the world cold, but this is a most joyful season, as any birth is joyful. Christmas, after all, celebrates a birth, and that feast falls within this period. The Jewish festival of Hanukkah celebrates the return of the sun's light with glowing candles.

I always save a special log to burn at the solstice, very much like a Yule log. I choose the roundest, most

---

TUNG CHIH
The Period of Winter Solstice

年

December 21–
    December 26, 1985

The period begins on Saturday, December 21, 1985, at 5:08 P.M., at the winter solstice.

Dec. 21–26, 1985

SAT.	SUN.	MON.	TUES.	
21	22	23	24	

perfect-looking log from solid hardwood like white oak, or especially applewood if I can get it. I make sure it's a generous log—one that will burn overnight.

When the log is burning, I watch its light, light that's been stored in the wood since sunlight fell on the leaves and added rings of new wood year by year. First the log's most recent years burn off, then older wood burns down. The last embers recall the sunlight that fell on the new sapling 40 or 50 years ago. That sun also warmed Hitler's Wehrmacht, burned up the Great Plains, lit up Yankee Stadium for Babe Ruth; now that light stored so long ago helps me celebrate the sun's swing back north in 1985.

 ## The Sunset Moves

Here's how to mark on a windowsill facing west the place where the sun sets. At the winter solstice, it sets farthest to the south (to the left as you look out the window). Use a nail or screw for a rear sight, then mark how the sunset point begins to travel to the right as days go by. The sunset on the spring and fall equinoxes occurs at the same place. Summer solstice sunset is farthest to the right, when the sun is directly over the earth's Northern Hemisphere.

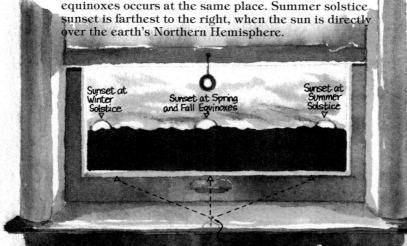

	WED.	THURS.
	25	26

Blessing the Apple Trees

In rural England, it was long a custom to bless the apple trees at this time of year. The ancient wassail was a part of this ritual, where people would visit a tree with a drink in hand, toast its health, take a drink, bless the tree, perhaps take another drink, then move on to the next tree. Today's trees are as much in need of our blessing as trees of old. Try this ritual yourself, as I did last year. I visited each of my five apple, two pear, two cherry, two apricot, and two plum trees in turn. I projected warm feelings of stewardship and encouragement onto them. And I saw them as fellow creatures that depended on me to make a go of it. It was very quiet and cold—a misty, frosty kind of day. The late afternoon light was failing. No one saw me standing quietly in the orchard, but I had a feeling of togetherness with those trees, the way you feel in a room with sleeping children.

The mind is like a snowflake. When it's cold, it's rigid and patterned. When it's warm, it's fluid. And when it' s hot, it evaporates.

Doctor Earth

Winter and Compost

Think for a moment that the rich, crumbly fin-ished compost you put on your garden was once green stalks, leaves, and flowers waving under a midsum-mer sun. Now, at the winter solstice, the cycle has turned and the stuff of summer has withered and lost its individuality in the homogenous humus of the compost pile.

The soil and nutrient cycle begins with finished compost, for it is biologically stable and full of plant

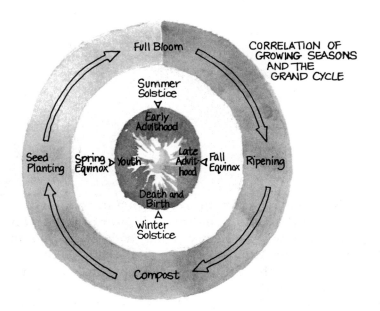

Full Bloom

Summer
Solstice
∇
Early
Adulthood

Seed
Planting

Spring
Equinox ▷ Youth

Late
Advlt-◁ Fall
hood   Equinox

Ripening

Death and
Birth
∆
Winter
Solstice

Compost

nutrients, a perfect material in which to start seeds in the spring. Compost, then, is the nadir of the grand cycle, the moment of death and immediate rebirth, like the very moment that we're celebrating: the winter solstice.

Walt Whitman saw the cleansing power of the earth in the compost heap. His poem "This Compost" ends thus:

> Now I am terrified at the Earth, it is that
>   calm and patient,
> It grows such sweet things out of such
>   corruptions,
> It turns harmless and stainless on its axis,
>   with such endless successions of diseas'd
>   corpses.
> It distills such exquisite winds out of such
>   infused fetor,
> It renews with such unwitting looks its prodigal,
>   annual, sumptuous crops,
> It gives such divine materials to men, and
>   accepts such leavings from them at last.

It's a nice idea to plant something in your own finished compost in the house on Winter Solstice Day, the natural new year. Last year my wife, Marilyn, and I planted Sugar Ann dwarf snap peas in a trough under the skylight. They grew weakly through January and delivered five or six minipods to us in late February and early March. Though only morsels, what morsels they were, full of sweetness and meaning.

✎ Winter's Tale ✎

Geese mate for life, and that applies to the wild as well as the domestic kind. Not far from our place in eastern Pennsylvania is a pond where a wild Canadian gander paired with a white domestic goose. The male was a strong flier, but the white goose limited her flying to occasional circles above the pond. As winter approached, the pair looked more and more disconsolate, especially after the last flight of wild geese had honked their way over the horizon. Then one day, at about winter solstice, they were gone. Much later, we found out the rest of the story from the lady who owned the pond.

The wild male got to migrate, all right, but because of his mate's limitations, the migration took them only as far as a mile and a half due south to a neighbor's pond, where they were seen to spend the winter. They returned to our friend's pond in the spring.

Dreams and Wishes

The holiday uproar is over. The days are short and cold. Peace and quiet return, along with the daily routine. The weather keeps us close to the hearth. It's a good time to catch up on reading in order to stir some new and different ideas into our minds.

HSIAO MAN
*The Period of
Lesser Cold*

找

December 27, 1985–January 9, 1986

The period begins on Friday, December 27, 1985, at 2:31 A.M., at the full moon.

Taking a cue from dormant and self-absorbed nature, it's a good time to reflect on the past year, or on our lives, to see what we've done with the time and made of ourselves. And here's the crucial question that leads to a very seasonal celebration: Now that we've finished with the old year, what do we want to do in the new one?

In our family, we always title our list of dream wishes, "Things I Want to Do This Year." Everyone in the family makes out a list of 10 or 12 New Year's Wishes, signs the list and folds it for secrecy. The lists are put in an envelope, which is filed away.

The next New Year's Day, the lists are taken out and read. How many of the things on the lists were accomplished? Who had the most wishes come true? How can each of us have more of our own wishes come true?

Wishing and thinking about new, exciting directions is time well spent. Young people especially need to identify and follow their dreams. A tradition of New

1
4

Dec. 27, 1985–Jan. 9, 1986

FRI.	SAT.	SUN.	MON.	
27	28	29	30	

Year's Wishes might help throw light on various paths into the future.

It helps to look at nature during this time of year. The world's face is being scrubbed, the slate wiped clean. New dreams and better gardens are possible only when the old have been washed away.

❧ Music to the Ears ❧

The winter wails are back. From somewhere far away, the train whistle slices through the frigid air. No leaves muffle the sound as it rolls over fields and hills. Hearing becomes acute in this atmosphere, as if the

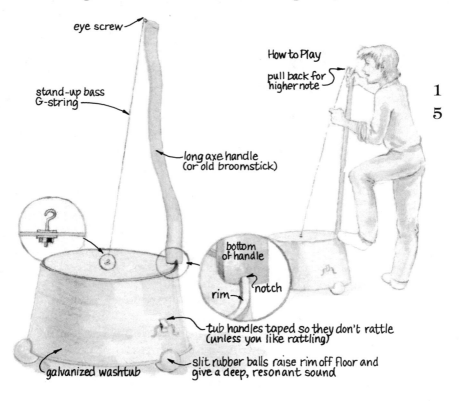

eye screw

stand-up bass
G-string

long axe handle
(or old broomstick)

How to Play

pull back for
higher note

bottom
of handle

rim   notch

tub handles taped so they don't rattle
(unless you like rattling)

galvanized washtub

slit rubber balls raise rim off floor and
give a deep, resonant sound

	TUES.	WED.	THURS.	FRI.
	31	1	2	3

faraway horn announces other, subtler sounds, if only we would listen.

It's a good time of year to play music, to write it, to sling it out on the countertop with spoons and whatever dishes and pots are handy. It's a good time to make a gut bucket. Follow the directions in the illustration on page 15.

I've made six or eight of these washtub basses over the years. I learned how from the bartender at a dude ranch, a little guy named Eddie who spent his winters in Florida and his summers at northern resorts.

Because this Period of Lesser Cold is one of reflection, listening to music is an appropriate way to celebrate. It sharpens our hearing. It quiets us and focuses our attention. Take that attention outside on a clear, cold day and *listen*. Pretend you're hearing a piece of very avant garde music, played by an orchestra of dogs, cars, airplane engines, wind, *vox humana*, and whatever else floats in on the breeze. There's real music there for sure.

∽ Recreate in the Snow ∽

Lovers of winter sports should be entering nirvana about now. In the North, ponds are frozen or freezing fast. Slopes are covered with snow in many regions.

A time of reflection, like this period, requires that the mind be still. One of the best things about sports and athletics is that you must learn to do them without thinking. A downhill skier, for example, had better not think *too* much on the way down—the sport forces one to put the brain on automatic pilot and enjoy the ride. Sports'll do that. And so will playing music. All the training brings the student to the point

SAT.	SUN.	MON.	TUES.	
4	5	6	7	

of letting go, whereupon the music comes flowing off the fingertips. The same thing happens when we speak. We long ago ceased to think about forming words, and they usually roll straight from mind to mouth.

Which reminds me of a memorable sled ride I once had. It was a good mile or more from the top of Neyhardt's Hill to the very bottom, where Kettle Creek runs. I must have been about 10 or 11, and I struggled to the top, pulling the sled. I looked, gulped, and launched out. Near the bottom of the steepest part of the hill the sled was going so fast that I knew I couldn't keep tight control anymore. The sled was flying and I flew with it. No thought was involved. The sled and I were one, and we shot down the snowy road in a white blur. When the sled slowed down a little, I remember taking over control again and steering it to a safe stop. Something physical, beyond the power of my mind to control, had taken over and shoved my intellect aside.

WED.	THURS.
8	9

Pink and Blue

The theme colors of the holiday season are green and red. Mid-spring's theme is green grass and yellow dandelions. Fall is hung with yellow, orange, and red bunting. The Period of Greater Cold is colored not with the saturated pigments of the warm seasons but with the most delicate pastel pinks and blues.

TA HAN
The Period of Greater Cold

過

January 10–January 25, 1986

The period starts on Friday, January 10, 1986, at 7:22 A.M., at the new moon.

This is the cold heart of winter. Nights are bitter. Even the goat nags to come in the house. The wood stove gulps logs. Just after dawn, light pink clouds float in a pale blue sky. In the evening, a pink glow from the setting sun spreads across the snow, while a soft slate blue appears in the hollows and shaded places. These are baby colors, infant colors, appropriate for the infancy of the year.

The pink and blue of morning promises more humane weather to come and reassures us that intense

Jan. 10–25, 1986

FRI.	SAT.	SUN.	MON.	
10	11	12	13	

cold has its benefits. For one thing, it beats back the organisms that are out to get us. Diseases, insects, and parasites in tropical countries are not chased into yearly dormancy by January weather and are the more fearful for it. In the temperate zones, the cold teams with the actinic sunlight to sterilize the soil over winter. Another benefit: Winter is invigorating, bracing. Its crisp, cold days keep us moving briskly along. And another: A good, deep snow cover slows soil erosion and moderates temperatures under the snow for tender plants and crops. And yet another: Alternate freezing and thawing crack apart tiny pieces of rock in the soil, reinvigorating cropped earth with fresh mineral nutrients.

Some seeds won't germinate and some plants won't flower unless they are frozen over a winter. People who've been raised in northern areas and transplanted to the Sun Belt for a few years start missing winter. Despite the grumbling that winter elicits, I think we would all miss it dearly should summer ever bloom eternal over the earth.

From deep within the cold heart of the inevitable winter, let's celebrate the miracle of blue ice and pink snow.

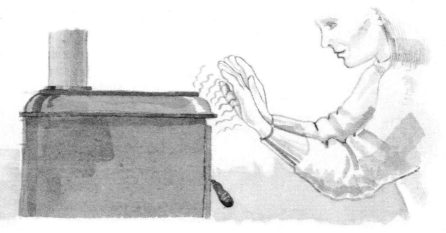

TUES.	WED.	THURS.	FRI.
14	15	16	17

Winter Time

Late lies the wintry sun a-bed,
A frosty, fiery sleepy-head;
Blinks but an hour or two; and then,
A blood-red orange, sets again.

Before the stars have left the skies
At morning in the dark I rise;
And, shivering in my nakedness,
By the cold candle, bathe and dress.

Close by the jolly fire I sit
To warm my frozen bones a bit;
Or, with a reindeer sled explore
The colder countries round the door.

When to go out, my nurse doth wrap
Me in my comforter and cap;
The cold wind burns my face, and blows
Its frosty pepper up my nose.

Black are my steps on silver sod;
Thick blows my frosty breath abroad;
And tree and house, and hill and lake,
Are frosted like a wedding cake.

Robert Louis Stevenson

SAT.	SUN.	MON.	TUES.	
18	19	20	21	

⊷ Cabin Fever ⊶

In the last weeks of January, the holiday season already seems remote. The weather has turned truly miserable, and the awful realization hits: You're sick of winter and the worst is yet to come. It's too cold to enjoy a walk. You're cooped up in the house without relief. Loved ones become maybe a bit too familiar. If only there were a way to get away and enjoy a moment alone. But there isn't. Your voice turns shrill, a little less rational. Your fuse shortens. At dinner, you plan to announce your impending move to Majorca, or the Cameroons, but all you say is, "Why do we live in a climate like this anyway? We don't have to live here."

It's cabin fever, all right. There are remedies. Here are a few tried-and-true cures:

—Move to Majorca, or the Cameroons.
—Get around to starting that double life you've always wanted to live.
—Go on a hunger strike until the kids agree to help out with the housework.
—Hibernate.
—Win the lottery.
—Count snowflakes.

When all the options are weighed, however, most of us realize there's no alternative to toughing it out. So why not put the time to good use? Perfume the sheets. Make the best dessert ever. The secret is to serve.

WED.	THURS.	FRI.	SAT.
22	23	24	25

❧ Ice Jewels ❧

Now that it's really cold, the ice jewels appear.
Sunlight, streetlights, car headlights—all glint off the
snow and ice that rime the world and set it afire.
You can see the glimmers when you walk—little
reflections from the myriad mirrored surfaces of the
ice crystals.

Diamond: You see a flash of fiery white and blue, or
intense pinpoints of starlight in the snow.
Sapphire: Rich, sapphire-blue color will glint
from the snow, then disappear.
Ruby: A rare ice jewel, the ruby-red flash is
usually seen in new-fallen snow at night when a
strong white light is reflecting from the drifts.
Emerald: Rare indeed. I'm not sure I've ever seen
an emerald glint. Keep your eyes open.
Topaz: A flash of light yellow is fairly common,
especially in strong reflected sunlight. Although I call
it topaz, it could be thought of as citrine or even
yellow sapphire.

**2
3**

Like jewels of stone, jewels of ice are many-
faceted. It's always amazed me that we can see light
reflected from such minute surfaces at all. Many
nights I have walked the length of our quarter-mile
driveway after a snowstorm, heading toward our
neighbor's white backyard light, and seen the jewels
sparkle and spill over one another, huge mounds of
tiny crystals flashing red, white, and blue as I walk.
Once every few years we get an ice storm that
coats every twig and branch in the trees, and all the
stems and stalks in the fields, with a layer of ice.
Then I see the ice jewelry: The trees are made of
glimmering glass. Bushes sparkle with necklaces of
pure quartz, set in the gold of sunlight. Although they
are worthless gems, dream jewels that will be gone
tomorrow, they are no less beautiful than real stones.

Sugartime

The signs are subtle, but the world is beginning to climb up and away from the deepest, darkest part of winter. The sun's a little bit brighter and stays abroad a few minutes longer.

LI CHHUN
The Period of Beginning of Spring

生

January 26–February 7, 1986

The period starts on Sunday, January 26, 1986, at 7:31 P.M., at the full moon.

Nature slaps the trees awake, gently stroking them with above-freezing temperatures during the day and smacking them with hard frosts at night. Within the trees, the sap begins to stir. Starches stored last summer are turned back into sugar and move with the rising sap. In the woods, unseen and unheard, the trees are charged with new life. I've stood in the woods on such days, ankle-deep in snow, and imagined the energy surging through the trees around me. I always end up thinking about maple syrup.

What a miracle! The trees themselves are fountains of sweetness! Early New England settlers, cut off from supplies of cane sugar, turned to the maple trees. They found the first run of sap to be the lightest, with the least maple flavor—a good thing, since otherwise all their sweet dishes would have tasted like maple. The lightest grade of syrup is still Fancy, the next lightest Grade A, and so on toward dark and mapley Grade C.

The trees perform alchemy to make their sugar: In the leaves, green chlorophyll molecules use free

2
4

Jan. 26–Feb. 7, 1986

SUN.	MON.	TUES.	WED.	
26	27	28	29	

electrons to splice carbon dioxide and water together. This sugar is pumped back down the leaves into the tree, to be stored as starch. The starch is reconverted to sugar at sap rising to feed the buds that will eventually pop open to make new leaves and manufacture more sugar.

Thoughts of impending spring can make our blood rise from winter's doldrums, too. In fact, the hemoglobin molecules in our blood are built very much like chlorophyll, except that they are built around atoms of iron, while chlorophyll uses magnesium. They perform analogous functions, but with mirror-image results: The trees use carbon dioxide as their raw material and give off oxygen; we use oxygen as our raw material and give off carbon dioxide in our breaths. Both trees and man respire, each using what the other discards.

Sugartime reminds us that the seas and winds rise in life's bodies, and that at the core, life is sweet. I can't think of a better way to celebrate it than by slathering a stack of buckwheat pancakes with real maple syrup on a frosty winter morning.

THURS.	FRI.	SAT.	SUN.
30	31	1	2

❧ Groundhog Day ❧

Perhaps because we long ago lost the link to Europe, Americans tend to trivialize the most solemn seasonal celebrations from the Old World. The meaning of Christmas recedes behind the mask of a jolly Santa Claus, ho-ho-ho-ing like the laughing gypsy on the funhouse roof. Similarly, Candlemas Day on February 2 is all but forgotten behind the yearly rush to see if Punxutawney Phil—a stuffed groundhog—sees his shadow.

But Candlemas, at its ancient root, was a celebration of the White Goddess, the ruler of heaven and earth in the Golden Age before Homer. The moon was her incarnation. It was time to consecrate the new fire, as the sun strengthened in the sky and the bright February moon kindled the night.

How remote the concept of gods and goddesses seems to us now. Ribald, short-tempered, cruel, and full of tricks, the ancient deities scampered in the skies of old, and we wonder at the naivete of our forebears. The ancients, however, had a different conception. The gods and goddesses were, among other things, archetypes for human states of being. When you were drunk, Bacchus was in you. When you were amorously aroused, Eros possessed you. Courage was the god in you, and beauty was the goddess.

The plants were inhabited by spirits, too. In Celtic religion, each god and goddess was a planet, sun, or moon. They were also associated with a tree or shrub and with a specific rune of the alphabet. Groves and gardens could be arranged—and often were—to carry hidden and sacred meanings through the god–plant–rune association. If only the god or goddess would then enter into you, your eyes might be opened to read the hidden messages in all of nature. And then

2
6

MON.	TUES.	WED.	THURS.	
3	4	5	6	

you would be wise, a priest or priestess, able to foretell and explain events.

It takes no leap of the imagination to see that scientists are our modern priesthood, reading the hidden messages of nature, foretelling and explaining events to the rest of us.

As we enter our gardens this year, let's look through ancient eyes and see what they saw. Then let's look with scientific understanding and see the processes science has described. And then let's drop our preconceptions and see what's really there.

	FRI.
	7

First Salad, Best Salad

Right about now, we always have our first spring salad. We've grown Witloof chicory—Belgian endive—roots the season before, and now we're forcing the roots to produce chicons—the nice, tight heads of creamy-yellow chicory that make such exquisite salads.

Each fall, I harvest the chicory roots and trim the tops to about an inch. Then I bury them in a 2-foot pit and cover it with bags of leaves and hay bales. In January, I gather some for forcing in the cellar, and by The Period of Beginning of Spring they're ready to eat. We slice them lengthwise, pour on a little oil and vinegar, and add a sprinkle of oregano. Nothing beats a fresh-picked salad of chicory in the middle of winter, especially when it's accompanied by just-grown alfalfa sprouts from the windowsill.

Broke Again

This year, let's celebrate being broke after paying off all the holiday bills. After all, "when you ain't got nothin', you got nothin' to lose," and "the best things in life are free."

For the kids: lolly-ices. Freeze a tray of ice cubes with a stick in each cube. The sticks are wrapped with a paper napkin and the ices licked until they're gone. Delicious.

For the adults: air champagne. Although short of finish and lacking any discernible qualities at all, air champagne has the virtue that it can be drunk by the gallon with no ill effects. The glasses can't break. But the toasts can be real and heartfelt.

A votre sante!

DRAWING GAME

Fold a sheet of paper into four panels. Four players take turns drawing a panel without knowing what's been drawn before, clued only by a few guidelines.

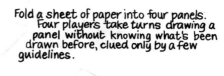

First person draws the top panel.

He or she makes guide marks on the next panel...

and folds the top drawing back over so the second person can't see it. Person #2...

does a drawing, opens the paper and makes the guide marks, then refolds it.

Person #3 uses the guide marks to draw a panel. Guide marks are made and the paper is folded and given to person #4. No one has seen any of the others' panels. When #4 is finished, the paper is unfolded and the whole picture is seen.

By Cometlight

Mark Twain came into the world in 1835, the year of Halley's Comet. He predicted that he would die in 1910, the year of its return. On April 20, 1910, Halley's Comet reached its perihelion—the point closest to the sun—and began to swing back toward the vast unknowns of interstellar space. The next day, April 21, Twain died. He obviously left with it. It's easy to picture Twain astride the comet, his white hair streaming behind like a tail, waving goodbye.

YU SHUI
The Period of the Rains

星

February 8–February 23, 1986

The period starts on Saturday, February 8, 1986, at 7:55 P.M., at the new moon.

30

Now Halley's Comet has returned again, reaching its perihelion during this period, on February 10. We can only wonder where it goes to pick up such geniuses, and hope that this time it brings us another humorist of Twain's caliber. Twain had the quality all genius shares: the ability to see things as they really are. He had a peculiarly American kind of jaundiced eye to boot. He knew that people's expectations for bliss in the afterworld, for example, are so limitless that they're a sin. In his "Visit to Heaven" (1906), one angel describes to another the rude awakening in store for a preacher when he finally gets to the Pearly Gates:

"For instance, there's a Brooklyn preacher by the name of Talmadge who is laying up a considerable disappointment for himself. He says every now and

Feb. 8–23, 1986

SAT.	SUN.	MON.	TUES.	
8	9	10	11	

then in his sermons that the first thing he's going to do when he gets to heaven will be to fling his arms around Abraham, Isaac, and Jacob, and kiss them and weep on them. There's millions of people down there on earth that are promising themselves the same thing. As many as 60 thousand people arrive here every single day that want to run straight to Abraham, Isaac, and Jacob, and hug them and weep on them. Now mind you, 60 thousand a day is a pretty heavy contract for those old people. If they were of a mind to allow it, they wouldn't ever have anything to do, year in and year out, but stand up and be hugged and wept on 32 hours out of the 24. They would be tired out and as wet as muskrats all the time. They're kind and gentle, but they ain't any fonder of kissing the emotional highlights of Brooklyn than you be."

Let's celebrate the return of Twain's comet and its unearthly light by seeing ourselves in bold relief, laughing at ourselves, regaining our sense of what's important, and cherishing our individual genius—as Mark Twain exemplified so well.

	WED.	THURS.	FRI.	SAT.
	12	13	14	15

By Cometlight

The comet comes but seldom, yet
    we recognize the place
That stands out clear before us
    when the comet shows his face.

By cometlight we see ourselves
    exactly as we are—
For that, we couldn't have enough
    of any star.

J.C.

❦ Under the Skylight ❦

I hope Halley's Comet shows in the east. That's
the direction we see through the 8 by 8-foot skylight
in our roof. When we start our parsley and onions in
flats under the skylight, the comet can shine on them.
These will go out into the garden in six to eight weeks
as thrifty little seedlings. In the meantime, we'll have
started everything else—from bell peppers to tomatoes.
From now until April, we sleep in a combination
bedroom/potting shed.

SUN.	MON.	TUES.	WED.	
16	17	18	19	

I'm interested to see how plants perform with a comet in their aspect. We know there's a relationship between the moon and plants' behavior, and it goes without saying that the sun makes plants do just about everything they do. Some people draw the line there and deny that other celestial bodies, like stars, could have any effect on earth's plants; others swear they have all kinds of effects. I'm not sure it makes a particle of difference whether stars do or don't have effects on plants. If they do, it's not in my power to stop it; if they don't, then I don't have to think about it. In either case, I've got to work with what I can affect.

I'm celebrating the return of the comet by planting a special garden of seedlings nurtured in late February and March by its overarching light. Not many peppers get to grow by cometlight.

THURS.	FRI.	SAT.	SUN.
20	21	22	23

❧ The Earliest Riser ❧

Although it's still cold, sleeping skunks have had enough of winter. You don't have to see one walk by to know the skunks are awake. With precious little to eat in February, skunks occasionally foray onto our front porch for a nibble of cat food. At such times, we enter and exit the house very carefully.

We have a black-and-white Tom among our cats, and once I thought I was pouring him a bowl of dry cat food. When he approached the bowl I saw that it wasn't Tom at all. It was a skunk. *Slowly* I tiptoed backwards, clutching the cat food bag in horror. If nice Mr. Skunk should become alarmed, there goes the neighborhood.

My dog did nothing except remove himself quite a distance from the porch and let me work it out alone. He'd been mousetrapped in the smeller too many times by those little black-and-white things. Considering how bad skunks smell to us, and that a dog's nose is up to 200 times more sensitive than ours, I didn't blame him a bit.

The skunk was oblivious to me, however. I stood a respectful distance away and watched him crunch happily on his cat food. He was my first spring visitor, the first animal up and abroad in the earliest time of the year. What a wonderfully effective defense he has—one so good that the skunk can be so mild-mannered, not afraid of anything, that he wanders onto the roads at night and expects the autos to get out of his way.

Hats off to this incredible creature—if only to cover our noses with.

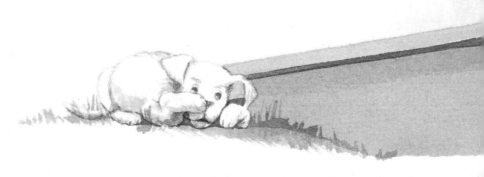

Be My Valentine

Be my Valentine. You know who you are. You're the ones who feed your birds. The ones who'll hold a just-born kitten to their breast to warm it while the mother cat delivers another. The ones who cry real tears when they accidentally kill an animal on the road.

My Valentines would be all the people whose first question is, "What can I do for you?" The ones who think ahead so they stay off other people's toes. The ones who care about clean water and endangered species and world hunger.

I want all the married people who remain wildly in love with their spouses for my Valentines. And all the ones who've loved and lost, yet still believe in love.

And finally, I want all those who trust from the heart without knowing why; who believe in magic; who forgive most grievous wrongs; who feel at home at home.

Mud Time

The ground freezes from the top down in November through January. By March, a waxing sun thaws it in the same way. For a time, then, before the thaw penetrates all the way through the frozen layer, water can't drain from the thawed surface and the soil turns to mud.

CHING CHE
The Period of
Awakening of Creatures 土

February 24–March 19, 1986

The period begins on Monday, February 24, 1986, at 10:02 A.M., at the full moon. It includes the new moon on Monday, March 10, at 9:52 A.M.

There was a time, early on in life, when mud was cause enough for a celebration. It squished. It held its shape well enough. It was especially wonderful when forced out between fingers and toes. Good mud could be made into pies. It was the season of the

36

MUD TIME
rain water — thawed layer — rain water →
frozen layer
permanently thawed layer

Feb. 24–Mar. 19, 1986

MON.	TUES.	WED.	THURS.	
24	25	26	27	

disappearing pie tins, and I can still remember the beautiful sight of a row of mud pies set out to bake in the sun.

Good mud also made good dirt bombs. These were ammo for the incessant warfare and skirmishes practiced by the kids in my neighborhood. Our soil was sandy, and handfuls of mud left to dry, then thrown like grenades, exploded on impact in a satisfying burst of dust, powder, and sand. Mothers sometimes wonder how their kids get so dirty. The answer on my block was dirt bombs.

But later come the years when mud is the enemy of the shoes you like so much. And when you get your first car stuck in the mud and just about tear out the transmission "rocking" it. This never works. Like a Chinese Finger Trap, it only gets you in deeper. And finally, as mud is replaced by money as the raw material of life, it becomes merely a nuisance.

Yet each of us remains ever a handful of mud with the breath of life in it. Mud is the sensitive goop out of which creatures arise and to which they eventually return. Mudpacks beautify and mud baths revivify. The earth is a healer, and we lose touch with it at our peril. Gardeners, especially, know what the earth can do.

This is Mud Time! Let's make one more mud pie for auld lang syne. Decorate the top with pebbles and sticks. Bake it in the sun for a day or two and then—in the style of the kids we once were—dump it without ceremony.

Angels We Have Heard on High

Church bells ring out the Angelus at the opening and closing of the day in many European countries. This call to prayer, heard throughout the villages and

	FRI.	SAT.	SUN.	MON.	TUES.
	28	1	2	3	4

outlying farms, was painted by Millet in a famous scene of peasants praying the Angelus, and the bells are almost audible in the picture.

In the eastern United States, the natural year opens with the return of the Canada geese in late winter and closes with their departure south in the late fall. This seasonal Angelus marks a definite change. If winter is a blanket that settles over the earth, then the geese draw it over us in the fall and lift it off in March. Behind the geese come the warming sun, the advancing lines of robins, and the popping crocuses.

If we have no Angelus bells, we have the geese, making their joyful noise, alternately sending the world to bed and waking it up.

38

WED.	THURS.	FRI.	SAT.	SUN.	
5	6	7	8	9	

❦ The Darkest Hour ❦

They say the darkest hour is just before dawn, and that's true for the period before spring begins. The ground turns to mud. The deepest snows I've ever seen have come in March. The wind howls through the month. Between the rains and the snowmelt, streams and rivers will flood. Temperatures swing between January and May. It's flu season. The winds dry the stalks and sticks of last summer's creations, and the countryside is turned to tinder. A scouring, scourging, and purging is taking place across the land. Our consolation is that upon this *tabula rasa* nature is sure to write large.

❦ The B-52s ❦

Sometime in this Period of Awakening of Creatures, the March fly emerges. Where he comes from I have no idea. He may have wintered-over in a crevice or hatched from an egg.

He's unmistakable. Although he looks like an ordinary housefly, he's darker, rougher, and about twice the size. He also flies at about half the speed. Like a lumbering Gotha bomber of World War I or the Flying Fortress of World War II, the fly moves with the deliberate speed of someone on a mission. His droning buzz can be heard half a room away. In my fantasies, he goes about distributing eggs for the season's fly population like a malevolent Easter Bunny. But then he would be a she. I'm left unsure.

I never see more than one of these harbingers of spring. One is all you need.

MON.	TUES.	WED.	THURS.	FRI.
10	11	12	13	14

∽ Sleepers Awake ∽

Though winter will take several curtain calls in
this period, the onion grass and wild garlic send up
their spears. The daylilies grow an inch of green
foliage to test the winter. The celandine forms a larger
rosette of scalloped leaves. Buds on the trees get fat.
Wild animals are up and abroad. Birds sound a new
note. It's not yet spring, but everyone is getting ready.

In the South, gardeners are planting spring crops.
In the mild mid-Atlantic zone, peas and onions go in.
In the colder places, the seeds must sleep awhile, but
the gardeners are wide awake and dreaming.

SAT.	SUN.	MON.	TUES.	WED.
15	16	17	18	19

Youth

They say that for the first half hour after the spring equinox, eggs will stand on their ends. Something to do with the spin of the earth as the sun crosses the equator. I like to think the eggs are *en pointe,*

CHHUN FEN
The Period of
Spring Equinox

兒

March 20–March 24, 1986

The period begins on Thursday, March 20, 1986, at 3:30 P.M., at the vernal equinox.

dancing out their joy in a rite of spring that all creatures in the Northern Hemisphere take part in. Once the flowers start opening, they multiply geometrically until we are buried in flowers in June. When spring begins, the kids and pups and cubs and kits are born. Seeds burst open with silent hoorays. Birds get nesty and hens start laying. New life suddenly appears everywhere, and everyone and everything is young.

Youth hasn't yet learned the limits of possibility, and so it frequently does the impossible. Its universe may be small — the block and the bedroom — but it contains all the power and potential of the grand universe at large. That youth can misuse the power should be no surprise, since even seasoned veterans of life misuse power. Youth has innocence, however, for an excuse. With a passion to grow and learn, youth pushes all the buttons and pulls all the levers, just to see what will happen.

Those of us who have passed beyond childhood's end can see that youth is a time of testing. Who can

42

Mar. 20-24, 1986

THURS.	FRI.	SAT.	SUN.	
20	21	22	23	

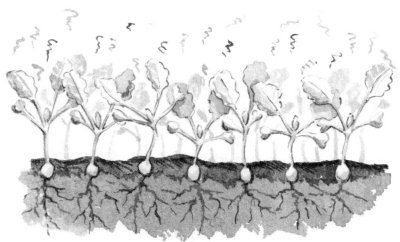

jump the farthest and run the fastest? Who's the
smartest? Who's got the talent? Gardeners may notice
that this kind of testing extends beyond the borders of
human life. The plants muscle and nudge one another
aside to jockey for position in the light. Below ground,
their roots are grasping every advantage they can get.
Spring growth is one vast race for sunlight and nutrients. The race goes to the lucky and the able.

Life's tough lessons must be relearned by every
generation. Having run the obstacle course, adults
offer the young much free advice on negotiating it. But
youth, put to the test, finds that it requires original
ideas and split-second decisions, and so relearns the
tough lessons by personal experience. Then the adults
shake their heads and say, "I told you so."

The best soil for young plants is compost—rich,
fertile, made from many elements. And the best
environment for the young has the same characteristics.
As in the garden, it's our job to prepare the best
seedbed and let the plant grow. It will be perfect if
perfection is in it.

MON.

24

❧ Spring Arrives ❧

One year I really saw the spring arrive. It was March 21, the first day of spring, and I was standing in front of my house. From the south, a line of robins—the first ones I'd seen that year—advanced directly across our property and headed off into the woods to the north. From where I stood, I could see about five or six of the birds on either side, about 20 feet apart, hopping, pecking, and fluttering northward at about 5 miles per hour.

In a few minutes they were gone, but the weather turned suddenly milder. The world smelled fresh and clean and the sunlight had a more mellow glint. I went back into the house. "Spring just arrived," I said.

❧ Winterspace, Summerspace ❧

When the weather drives us indoors in the fall, we enter a mental winterspace. We focus inside, on smaller places, more concentrated work. Winter is confinement, with a psychological feel all its own.

When the sun returns in the spring, we burst out-of-doors and begin to expand into summer's limitless rooms and airy houses. A part of our being begins to live outdoors again. Our daily rituals now include walks to the apple trees and the crocus beds to keep tabs on the progress of spring. It is now, at the equinox, that we move out of the living room and find more room for living.

Spring Chorale

My home is on the westward side of a high hill. From its top, I can see 50 miles or more across the valley to the east. In winter, the valley's half million people, its three cities and their suburbs, and the far-away tracery of several superhighways lie gray and quiet before me—a scene from a black-and-white silent film.

CHHING MING
*The Period of
Clear and Bright*

水

March 25–April 8, 1986

The period begins on Tuesday, March 25, 1986, at 10:02 P.M., at the full moon.

Winter attenuates our sense impressions. The smells of the earth disappear with the stinging frosts. Our fingers and toes become too numb to feel. Color drains out of the world, and the sounds of a lively, bustling earth are gone.

Spring, however, returns our senses to us one by one.

It's in this Period of Clear and Bright that we get our hearing back. It starts when the chickadees sing a noticeably different tune before taking off for the north country for the summer. New bird songs are heard, including the robin's familiar "cheer-up!" Geese continue their noisy fly-overs.

A few early-foraging bees visit the crocuses and *Scilla siberica,* taking home baskets of orange or blue pollen, respectively. Other insects buzz in the warm, sheltered places that catch the southern sun. The grass colors up and begins to grow, softening the hard, metallic quality of winter's sounds.

Mar. 25–Apr. 8, 1986

TUES.	WED.	THURS.	FRI.	
25	26	27	28	

Also in this period, I listen every day for the sound I love the most—the spring peepers. Through the last half of March, I usually listen in vain. Sometime in early April I'll hear just one peeper, but each day the chorus grows until the woods are alive with their sound. More than a symphony, more even than a Bach fugue, this natural music thrills me with its joy, hope, and beauty. The hylas' notes are icy pure. Thousands of frogs singing in counterpoint, surging like waves breaking on a shore, incessantly urge the world to wake up.

Strangely, although conditions for them are perfect, there were no hylas in our woods when we moved here. My wife, Marilyn, in her direct way, did something about it that first year. She stopped along a country road where they were singing, caught a few of the tree frogs and turned them loose below the house in the wet part of the property.

The next spring we did hear a few hylas singing. And the next year, a few more. Now we can stand on the front porch and hear their mighty chorus each year. What an incredibly beautiful gift those few frogs turned out to be.

Let's celebrate the return of sound and color by keeping a sharp eye and a cocked ear. Beauty is often found small, but the rewards are large. Besides the obvious colors and sounds, there's more to our sense impressions than meets the eye or ear.

	SAT.	SUN.	MON.	TUES.
	29	30	31	1

Cleansing

These are days to hang the blankets and comforters like bunting from windows. The winter's dust and dirt is shown the door. Windows sparkle. Spring cleaning transforms the dim recesses of an overused house into sweet-smelling rooms filled with buttery sunlight.

Outside, bees are making their cleaning flights, dropping a winter's worth of metabolic wastes before resuming their foraging and nursery duties. Besides the garden bulbs, they'll find the pussy willows are open for business.

Spring tonics cleanse the blood and body. Most old recipes call for seven bitter spring herbs. We make a tea from burdock root, a few violet leaves, stinging nettles (boiling them removes the irritating formic acid in their leaves), mustard leaves or flower shoots, dandelion leaves, daylily shoots and roots, and wild onions. If the stinging nettles are left out, the other ingredients can be chopped and added to a salad.

Our personal interiors can always use a sprucing up. Grudges, anxieties, bad habits, worries—toss them out! Leave nothing in the heart that isn't fresh, clean, and beautiful. It's spring!

Spring Break

Too many buds
of all kinds and colors.
Too much sun
on too little cover.

J.C.

WED.	THURS.	FRI.	SAT.	
2	3	4	5	

A Bow to the Rising Sun

Of all the official gifts this country has ever received, perhaps most thoughtful and beautiful is the planting of thousands upon thousands of ornamental cherry trees along the Tidal Basin in Washington, D.C., the gift of the Japanese people.

Each spring at about this period, the trees explode into clouds of pink blossoms that overwhelm the visitor with a sudden burst of color against the winter-gray landscape of stone, water, and grass. We are indeed indebted to the Japanese for understanding our need and filling it with such beauty.

SUN.	MON.	TUES.
6	7	8

New Green

One of my favorite places is the Museum of Modern Art in New York City, where each visit always culminates in the appreciation of the magnificence of a painting—one I may have seen dozens of times before without more than general regard.

KU YU
The Period of Grain Rain

木

April 9–April 22, 1986

The period begins on Wednesday, April 9, 1986, at 1:08 A.M., at the new moon.

On one visit, *The Last Confederate Soldier* by Larry Rivers was such a painting. I looked at it as I had many times before, but suddenly I noticed the subtle interplay of gray and blue and the bits of red-oranges that Rivers used to set off the more somber tones. And then I discovered a thousand masterful things about it. Another time, I was struck by a painting of a spring wheat field by a Russian artist. In the foreground, a hillside glowed with new green, intensifying as it crested the hill in the sunlight until the green became too intense to be natural—became supernatural, in fact. Something about it wouldn't let me go. The green became a mesmerizing emerald light that expressed all the hope and joy of a world resurrected. That was 15 years ago.

Since then, living mostly in the rolling hills of eastern Pennsylvania, I've slowly become aware of another transcendent green—this one found in nature, not on a canvas. This green appears at a particular moment in spring. Marilyn and I call it The Day.

Apr. 9–22, 1986

WED.	THURS.	FRI.	SAT.	
9	10	11	12	

Sometime after the grasses and grains green up, the trees break bud and begin to grow leaves. These new leaves need some time to develop enough chlorophyll to turn a rich summer green. At first, they're a light yellowish-white, quickly turning to light yellow-green. At about this time there'll come a day of low humidity and brilliant sunshine. As I drive home in the evening, the westering sun pours its light onto the hilltops, and there it is! The hills light up with a golden glow. Like the green light that leapt into the supernatural in the painting, the hilltops reach a color intensity that is either seen at that moment or missed for another year. Tomorrow, the leaves will be a little too green.

Let's celebrate The Day by keeping our eyes open for it and, when it occurs, capturing it with our hearts. People do see it—the Russian painter, for instance, and poets like Robert Frost. Here's Frost on this phenomenon:

Nature's first green is gold,
Her hardest hue to hold.
Her early leaf's a flower;
But only so an hour.

SUN.	MON.	TUES.	WED.
13	14	15	16

Daffy-Down-Dilly's come to town
In her green dress and yellow nightgown.

Mother Goose

✑ Baseball ✑

There are two ways to look at baseball, which is suddenly all over our radios, TVs, and newspapers. The first way is from outside, from the stands. There you see the big game: outfielders, infielders, batter, pitcher, catcher; everybody moving, trying to score, shagging flies.

The other way is from inside the game, where you see the little game: the duel between pitcher and batter. The pitcher tries to fool the batter, throwing him a curve when he expects a fastball. The batter tries to figure what's coming and swings at the spot where he thinks it'll be. The big game serves the little game. The best thing that ever happened for fans was the centerfield TV camera that lets us focus on the trajectories of the pitches.

There's a big and little game to gardening, too. The grandstanders see the food and flowers flowing out of the garden, the overall look with masses of beets, rows of peas, a stand of broccoli or delphiniums. The little game is between the gardener and each plant. The plants are individuals — this one may need weeding, that one may need feeding — but they all require special care to produce the fountains of food that bystanders applaud.

There's only one way to celebrate baseball: Get up a little game in the vacant lot. If there aren't enough players, let the dog play second base.

THURS.	FRI.	SAT.	SUN.	
17	18	19	20	

⇔ A Time to Plant ⇔

Now is the time to plant leaf and fruit crops — anything that bears its edible parts aboveground. From the new moon to the full moon, the moon is waxing, and scientific studies have shown that many of these plants germinate and grow better during a period of waxing moon. Plant anything that can stand some late frosts. Plant root crops during a waning moon.

MON.	TUES.
21	22

⚘ Bluebirds ⚘

This is the time the bluebirds return to the northeastern states. But they never return for me. I haven't seen one in nearly 30 years. The last one I saw, I held in my hand, a spot of blood beaded on her red breast. I'd shot her with my BB gun.

It makes me feel sick to write about it. I realized at that moment how mindlessly cruel I had been with that damned gun. What beauty I had wantonly destroyed. And from that day to this, I have not shot another bird, although I've fed a passel of them.

Shortly after that painful incident, a terrible frost in the southeastern U.S. killed a whole generation of bluebird nestlings. Of those that survived, many were

kicked out of their haunts by starlings and killed by pesticides sprayed on woodlands to control pests like gypsy moths.

We've built bluebird houses and placed them around our garden, but since that day I was crushed by guilt, I've never seen that flash of beautiful blue and the warm, cheerful red breast, or heard the wonderful bluebird voices singing about happiness.

I don't know if I'll ever see a bluebird in this life, although I've known a lot of happiness. But sometime, when I've earned it, there'll come a vision. As it says in the old World War II song, "There'll be bluebirds over the white cliffs of Dover tomorrow, just you wait and see."

Love in Bloom

This period is certainly one of the most beautiful in all the year. Temperatures in most of the country turn balmy. The dead trees, which stood black and quiet all winter, suddenly burst into bloom and are filled with bees.

LI HSIA
*The Period of
Beginning of Summer*

April 23–May 7, 1986

The period begins on Wednesday, April 23, 1986, at 7:46 P.M., at the full moon.

The bee is the tree's true love. The perfume of an apple tree may be pleasant to us, but it's meant for the bee. Our artists may paint the lovely blossoms on a bough, but the blossoms are there to enchant the bee. Ultraviolet light, which the bee can see but we can't, shows patterns and markings of flower petals that provide direction and placement for incoming bees. For its part, the bee gets something of ultimate value: food, the stuff of life itself. For its part, the tree gets pollinated, which eventuates in the production of seed, the tree's ultimate goal. In getting its heart's desire, a true lover always gives the other *its* heart's desire.

Does a tree have any idea how beautiful it is dressed up in silky petals all pink and white, wearing its spring perfume? Love starts like that, too. But some people are so fond of the beauties of the blooming phase that they don't wait to experience the fruit.

The yearly pageant of sexual reproduction in the orchard gives us all the clues and inspiration we need

Apr. 23–May 7, 1986

WED.	THURS.	FRI.	SAT.	
23	24	25	26	

to conduct a benign human love affair. The tree and its pollinator not only benefit from the relationship, it is life itself to them. In taking, they are giving. In giving, they are taking. And the tree and the bee, while entirely separate entities, are interdependent, and this interdependence creates a living system that is both tree and bee in one.

When the trees themselves are blooming, we are surely in the fat of the year and as close to heaven as we get in this world. Let's use the occasion to remind ourselves that true love is not realized by becoming anyone else's servant, but by taking what we need from the other in such a loving way that they burst into bloom at our approach.

	SUN.	MON.	TUES.	WED.
	27	28	29	30

❧ Mulches ❧

The weeds are tiny now, but their relentless onslaught has begun. If you use a hoe, the motto is get 'em young and get 'em often. The best way to deal with weeds, however, is to smother them with mulch in April or May.

Here are some of the classic garden mulches:

Black Plastic: Great for melons and squashes, and sweet potatoes, too.

Spoiled Hay: Good for smothering paths and beds. Can be weedy and seedy.

Grass Clippings: A championship mulch with—usually—no weed seeds.

Leaves: Especially when matted together, a superior mulch.

Shredded Bark: Great-looking mulch for flower beds.

Peat: Weeds poke up through this stuff too easily. I stopped using it.

Old Rugs and Carpets: They're great, but just make sure that you remove them before they disintegrate, or you'll be finding bits of them in the garden soil for years.

THURS.	FRI.	SAT.	SUN.	
1	2	3	4	

Hooray, Hooray, the First of May

The first of May comes draped in tradition and very different meanings. Its most urgent meaning is as the international distress signal: Mayday! May Day is also a holiday for workers in Socialist and Communist countries, and the occasion for making speeches that tend to make us uncomfortable. It is also, of course, a festive rite of spring in Britain and the United States. This tradition began with the ancient Greek fertility festival of the Great Mother, and came down to Britain either through early migrants from the eastern Mediterranean or through Rome, or maybe both. It came here with British settlers.

In earlier days, there was a maypole—originally a tree, later a pole, decked out with leaves and garlands of flowers. Ribbons hung down from the top and were interwoven around the pole in intricate patterns by dancers, with the pattern reflecting the dance. In some rites, one girl was selected Queen of the May to represent the fertile spirit of spring that the ancients called the Magna Mater.

Let's celebrate this beautiful season by going a-maying. I've never been sure exactly what this means, but I think of walking through a blooming meadow with a lover, finding a spot to enjoy the sun, twining flowers in each other's hair, listening to the birds and the bees . . . that kind of thing.

MON.	TUES.	WED.
5	6	7

⋙ Tulips ⋘

All winter they've hidden under the ground in their bulbs, but now the tulips are up and opening their cheery cups. Our *Praestans fusilliers* add a welcome spot of red to the blues and yellows of the other bulbs.

The tulip is the veritable symbol of Holland and is well-used in Pennsylvania Dutch motifs. It was the first flower we learned to draw in kindergarten—the same shape also serving as an eggshell for the yellow chicks we mass-produced from stencils.

The flower originated in highland Iran and the Caucasus, where it's an inconspicuous spring meadow flower. Hybridizers and breeders early on cultivated it to produce marvelous variations in color and shape. In Holland in the 17th century, tulips became collectors' items and the objects of financial speculation. So wild did the trading in tulips become that fortunes were made and lost overnight.

But one cannot serve both God and Mammon. When tulipmania broke and prices returned to inexpensive levels, the tulips remained just as beautiful as before.

60

On the Beginning of Summer

Summer is icumen in.
Lhud singe cucu.
Bullock starteth
Ond bucke verteth
Ond lhud singe cucu.

Early Middle English Song

6
1

The Flowering

Now that the trees have led the way by blossoming, as if to say that flowers are a great idea, the earth itself bursts into bloom. Most of the flowers are old friends returning for another year: primrose, lilacs, bluebells, sea pinks, cranesbill, and so many others. It's been just about a year since I've seen them, and a year is just long enough to forget how much more beautiful they are in person than in memory.

HSIAO MAN
The Period of
Lesser Fullness of Grain 美

May 8–May 22, 1986

The period begins on Thursday, May 8, 1986, at 5:10 P.M., at the new moon.

To understand how much flowers mean to us, just imagine the world without flowers—everything else the same, but no blossoms anywhere. It would be an unrelieved wilderness of green and gray, black and brown. Spring would be a soft green tide instead of the phosphorescent fountain of colors that is bubbling out of the soil around us. Flowers, especially perennials that return year after year, give us something to look forward to with hope.

The perennials return in an orderly procession, called forth from their persistent roots at their appointed times. As the flowers parade through the seasons, their colors and forms keep changing but their beauty and optimism remain. Such gardens are always different and yet always the same. This year's clump of campanula is the same one as last year's clump, but all the foliage and flowers have been renewed.

Last year's foliage and blooms have fallen to the

May 8–22, 1986

THURS.	FRI.	SAT.	SUN.	
8	9	10	11	

ground and decayed to feed the roots that make this
year's display. The past ever lays an immoderate feast
for the present, and the present, if it is wise, chooses
carefully and not too much.

Flowers are a rather late development in the
evolution of plants. For billions of years, there were no
flowers. Perhaps they didn't appear until nature had
evolved beings that could appreciate them. They have
their practical aspects, but for people they are nature's
fragile decorations, jewelry made of spring's warm
breath, droplets of color that pull all the background
colors together and give them life. They grow in
profligate profusion everywhere, from all kinds of
plants with all kinds of functions.

The best thing about flowers—the part that makes
the heart sing—is that they really don't need to be at
all.

Although they have no purpose for us but beauty,
what would we do without them? Let's celebrate their
contribution to our lives by planting a bed of perennials and allowing a few more of these wonderful
creatures to exist.

	MON.	TUES.	WED.	THURS.
	12	13	14	15

Good and Bad

Good and bad and right and wrong,
Wave the silly words away;
This is wisdom: to be strong;
This is virtue: to be gay.
Let us sing and dance until
We shall know the final art,
How to banish good and ill
With the laughter of the heart.

James Stephens

❧ Dandelions ❧

6
4

There are lawns and gardens where not a single
dandelion grows. The gardeners uproot them as soon
as they reveal themselves by their golden heads.
Some gardeners are quite fanatical about it, and in the
rarefied circles of the horticultural elite, dandelions in
the garden are akin to roaches in the cupboard.

I can understand it. The bright yellow leopard's
bane in my perennial garden is always shouted down
by the even more brilliant yellow of the dandelions.
The subtleties of garden color schemes could be
easily obscured by the color intensity of too many of
these weeds.

While I understand the dandelion fanatics, I don't
cotton to the idea myself. At this season, I've driven
past whole hillsides glowing gold with dandelions.
Achieving that effect with leopard's bane would be a
herculean task. Whether in field or lawn, dandelions'
sheer exuberance conquers all.

FRI.	SAT.	SUN.	MON.	
16	17	18	19	

PLANTAIN ROCKETS

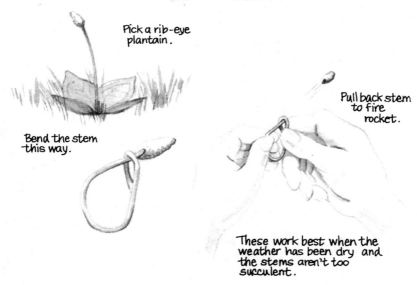

Pick a rib-eye plantain.

Bend the stem this way.

Pull back stem to fire rocket.

These work best when the weather has been dry and the stems aren't too succulent.

65

After all, dandelions give us our first spring salads with their icy-bitter young leaves so full of vitamins. Their flower heads have made wine for many a household. Children delight in blowing the seed heads away, making floating fairies and seeding the territory for next year's crop.

I've noticed that the burdock plant makes burrs with tiny grappling hooks just perfect for catching in the hair of animals. Could the burdock have evolved these structures to make wide dispersal by fur possible? Maybe the dandelions evolved their puffs just for children's breaths and their stalks as handles for children to grasp as they swing bunches of seed heads in wide arcs and float the seeds onto the breeze.

	TUES.	WED.	THURS.
	20	21	22

❧ Boomers ❧

Thunderstorms return to the northern states now.
Electricity again crackles from earth to sky and runs
amok among the clouds. The dog claws desperately at
the front door to be let in, then cowers under the
kitchen table as the thunder rolls by. I remember
cowering in my bed at night as a child, pleading with
heaven to spare me.

Since then I've seen too much of life and death to
be troubled by thunderstorms anymore. Now they are

exhilarating—wild tempests that roar with laughter—
fire in the sky—power of the earth.

    I try to share this point with the dog. He refuses
to believe me. I sneer at him for being such a baby.
But then the phone rings and I have a moment of fear,
based on the times I've heard fearful things over the
phone—bolts of fate's lightning from the blue that
changed my life forever in an instant. If the dog can
sense fear, even so slight a flash of fear as that, then it
is his turn to laugh at me.

Brides and Grooms

This long period covers the last week in May and the first three weeks of June: the time when couples tie the knot. The amorous stirrings that took young men's fancies and ladies' hearts in early spring have advanced far enough toward rapture that marriage breaks out all over.

MANG CHUNG
The Period of
Grain in Ear

婚

May 23–June 20, 1986

The period begins on Friday, May 23, 1986, at 3:45 P.M., at the full moon. It includes the new moon on Saturday, June 7, at 9:01 A.M.

68

Marriage may be a more mysterious affiliation than most of us suspect. The young man or woman who is still darting from experience to experience, trying everything out, discovering his or her likes and dislikes, is a questionable candidate for marriage in my book. A crucial component for success in marriage is that the partners know who they are. That is, they have matured into an acceptance of themselves as they are and a willingness to make choices based on that knowledge. Marriage can then be the union of two self-realized persons into the parts of an organic whole. Such a union, if it bears fruit, produces a husband and a wife.

In true marriage, both partners know what it means to be husband and what it means to be wife. Personality is not submerged; it's augmented and made whole. Love is a seed that's planted at the altar in hopes that it will grow. The seed will be watered diligently in the beginning with kindnesses and

May 23–June 20, 1986

FRI.	SAT.	SUN.	MON.	
23	24	25	26	

consideration, or it will dry out and die. If love does sprout, it will be handled tenderly in the early years or again it will die. Love will grow only in an atmosphere of trust. Both partners must husband it toward maturity, and that takes sacrifice beyond the expectations of most people entering marriage. Both partners must be wife—giving birth to love in their hearts and cherishing it forever.

When love matures and real marriage endures, it is tangible and sturdy, and its fruit is food for the souls of the partners. In this season of brides and grooms, let's hope they all turn into husbands and wives, and let's celebrate the period by finding new ways to nurture our own partners, children, gardens, or whoever comes to us in need.

Words to Live By

Never follow a banjo act with a banjo act.

Herbert Boyer

6
9

TUES.	WED.	THURS.	FRI.	SAT.
27	28	29	30	31

⤳ Wild Strawberries ⤳

Once I took a friend to a spot I know where wild strawberries grow. We wound through the woods on an old path and picked our way carefully through wild rose bushes into an old meadow full of second-growth bushes and half-grown trees. On the far side were the strawberries, but on the path ahead of us sat a big eastern box turtle, his neck craned to see us, his jaws stained strawberry red, with a big berry hanging from one side of his mouth. The year before I had obviously beaten the turtle to the patch, because I'd picked a good quart, but this year he'd beaten me. I had to look elsewhere for my berries.

I never realized what riches I had as a kid. The meadows immediately around my boyhood home were thick with strawberries. I'd gather a pint in five minutes and pour the berries, still sun-warm, over a dish of vanilla ice cream. This is, believe me, the very best tasting thing in the world.

A wild strawberry has all the taste of a big commercial berry, but it's crammed into a package one-tenth the volume. That means a single handful of wildings has the same amount of flavor as ten handfuls of cultivated berries.

The French may praise their *fraises* and the Italians applaud their *fragolini,* but I've tasted them all and nothing comes close to the wild strawberries of the eastern U.S.

They are the first fruit of the new year, and as "first fruit," a suitable offering. If the Good Lord ever came to claim this gift of nature, He'd have to beat the turtles, the birds, and the kids. Good luck.

SUN.	MON.	TUES.	WED.	THURS.	
1	2	3	4	5	

7
1

≈ Compound Creature ≈

The beehive is a compound creature whose cells
are individual bees. What a sublime strategy for
reaching a million flowers with their million tiny
drops of nectar: a beast with 10,000 tongues!

	FRI.	SAT.	SUN.	MON.	TUES.
	6	7	8	9	10

Everyone into the Pool

In this period, the water in lakes and ponds warms enough for swimming. There are some scientists who see evidence that man is descended from an aquatic mammal; for example, the cold diving reflex that shuts down the body's systems and which saved the life of a four-year-old boy who slipped under Lake Michigan for 20 minutes in January 1983. Or the fact that our ears can close from the inside (ever notice how hearing diminishes when we yawn?).

There is a bit of the otter in human beings. Swimming and diving may come as naturally as

WED.	THURS.	FRI.	SAT.	SUN.	
11	12	13	14	15	

walking. We expect children to walk. We don't expect them to innately know how to swim. And so they don't, and learn fear of the water. I wonder how many lives have been lost because of this attitude.

The water is not *too* warm at this season, however, and we're confronted with the old agonizing choice: get wet slowly, reducing but prolonging the shock, or quickly, intensifying but shortening it. It's the same choice that confronts someone with a piece of adhesive tape that must come off a hairy leg or arm.

This year, let's celebrate our first swim by getting wet the right way—doing the best cannonball we can.

MON.	TUES.	WED.	THURS.	FRI.
16	17	18	19	20

Young Adulthood

What is it that has the body of a man, the mind of a child, the stomach of a dog, the good sense of a doorknob, and the habits of a billy goat? A normal 21-year-old American male, you say? How right you are!

But nature, with exquisite foresight, set it up that way. Young adulthood is the time of peak sexual potency and reproductive prowess. The blood runs hot in one's twenties, but we can hardly blame the young because nature turns up their thermostats.

The summer solstice is the young adulthood of the year, and nature's turned up the thermostat in the natural world, too. The weather turns hot, forcing excesses of weed growth, molds, fungi, insects — nature is playing her big hand now, betting that all her creatures will pollinate, fertilize, and divide their way toward the next generation. To attract their pollinators, plants flower. In humankind, nature also assures reproduction by adorning young adults with physical attractiveness.

Just as young adulthood involves sowing the seeds of the new generation, it also means making choices and germinating ideas that will color the rest of the person's life. At the beginning of the journey, a fork in the road leads to two different worlds. Later in

TUNG CHIH
The Period of
Summer Solstice 日

June 21–July 6, 1986

The period begins on Saturday, June 21, 1986, at 11:30 A.M., at the summer solstice. It includes the full moon on Sunday, June 22, at 10:42 P.M.

June 21–July 6, 1986

SAT.	SUN.	MON.	TUES.	
21	22	23	24	

the journey, the forks usually lead only to different parts of the same world.

Casual choices are later seen to have been of crucial importance. Yet who could have known at the time how important they were? Could it be that the impulsiveness and irrationality of young adulthood unhook the conscious, safe, rational mind from decision-making too important for it to handle by itself? There is a side of us that's like the sea: We see only the surface with our conscious minds, but underneath lies a whole world of marvels. Perhaps we get help from that unseen world at this critical time of life.

Nature urges each creature to sow its seed where it will—not to figure out the costs and benefits of attraction, but to follow the infatuations that emerge from the depths of the heart. While this tendency has

	WED.	THURS.	FRI.	SAT.
	25	26	27	28

caused young people no end of trouble, it has also catalyzed many beneficial leaps forward into the unknown.

New conceptions always lie buried in the unknown like gems within rock. Only those who risk failure can reach them and pry them loose. Even those who fail are praiseworthy for having tried. Our new conceptions are always the cause of our greatest celebrations. In this season of summer solstice, when so much of the next generation of creatures is conceived, let's be thankful that the torch passes with such profound joy and pleasure.

∞ Midsummer's Eve ∞

For me, Midsummer's Eve conjures up the image of a group of sylphs in pastel gauze dancing in a pool of moonlight, while from nearby bushes several jocular and randy fauns look on. Shakespeare had the faeries' and imps' affairs all mixed up with those of humans on this night in his *Midsummer Night's Dream.* The festival itself seems a little mixed up, as it occurs on June 23, just a day or so after the summer solstice. One would think midsummer would be August 5, halfway to the autumn equinox.

But if we conceive of "summer" as the whole period of growth in the natural year, then June 23 falls just halfway between the start of spring on March 21 and the start of autumn on September 21. It is high noon in the natural year. Indeed, the sun is directly overhead and at its strongest. The pace of growth is most frantic. Only later, when the seeds are set and the mad rush to find a mate is over, will the world settle down into the comfy, lazy days of ripening summer.

SUN.	MON.	TUES.	WED.	
29	30	1	2	

Now the dance of life is in its crescendo, and on Midsummer's Eve it reaches the climax of the crescendo. In legend and lore, and perhaps in field and garden, the "other folk" appear. As every tale tells, they can't resist a good party.

The way to celebrate Midsummer's Eve is to throw an outdoor party. Just make sure you invite the faeries, even if they don't come.

One hard look can close the book that lovers love to see.

Robert Graves

	THURS.	FRI.	SAT.	SUN.
	3	4	5	6

7
8

✑ Fireflies ✑

A visitor from Europe once told me that the most amazing thing about America was the fireflies, unknown in his country. People who live in the cities or suburbs know them as occasional insects, flashing here and there in lawns and bushes. But the country person knows them in their profusion. I've seen a valley full of them in West Virginia, so lit up it looked like Manhattan from the air. And there's a marsh a mile from my house where the local residents often have company at this time of year so everyone can sit on their deck and watch a hundred thousand flashes at once. Speaking of displays. I've read about fireflies in South America that line the banks of rivers and flash on and off *in unison.*

I like them best, though, when they are thickest near the tops of trees on starry nights. To my eyes, it looks as though the stars continue into the trees and even down to earth, where they hide themselves in the meadow grass and wait for a child to catch them.

✑ Fireworks ✑

"I'd rather set off one piece of fireworks myself than watch a whole display someone else sets off," said the TV interviewer to the fireworks expert. He's not alone. What is it about people, especially men, that sets them giggling when something goes boom? Possibly the giggle or shout is an outlet for the tension of being startled. Fireworks wake us up, and as someone once said, the price of liberty is eternal vigilance.

The Berries

Now the berries, which have been swelling inconspicuously on their bushes throughout June, turn ripe. In the garden, the gooseberries become pink and soft and ready for the jam pot. The red and black raspberries hang like candy jewels from their canes. The black and red currants are ready. In the fields and along woods' edges, the wild berries have soaked up enough sun to produce a natural harvest that dwarfs the garden output, although they're hidden beneath hedges and in seldom-visited corners of the hay fields.

Because the wild berries are sweeter and more flavorful than the cultivated kind, I always go berrying. I like to do this alone, on a sunny July day when it's too hot to do anything else.

I start by going out for black raspberries around the end of the first week in July. The mornings are usually cool enough, and I grab the Chinese wicker basket that holds a gallon.

My forays always follow a pattern. At first, I find bushes with only a few berries on them. Wandering over the fields and along the forest edges, I come to more remote patches where the black raspberries are thicker. After about two hours or so, I will suddenly turn the corner of a hedgerow and find a mother

HSIAO SHU
The Period of
Lesser Heat

果

July 7–July 20, 1986

The period begins on Monday, July 7, 1986, at 11:55 P.M., at the new moon.

July 7–20, 1986

MON.	TUES.	WED.	THURS.	
7	8	9	10	

lode—a long stretch of bushes loaded with perfectly ripe fruit. From the mother lode I will pick in a half hour as many berries as I've picked in two previous hours. Soon I'll have a good gallon and start home, becoming aware for the first time that I am scratched, bug-bitten, drenched with sweat and perfectly satisfied to be that way. Home comes the mighty hunter of berries, loaded down, successful.

The strange part is that when I go berrying, I rarely eat a berry. I've been with berry pickers who eat as many as they pick. They never fill a gallon, and the berries they do take home are always the second choice since the best go galloping down their gullets. I'll eat berries off the bush anytime except when picking on Berry Day. It takes discipline to spend three or four muggy, buggy hours tramping miles in hopes of finding a mother lode. I'm convinced that if I didn't pick the less-endowed bushes, I would never be able to find the mother lode at all. It's the process of picking the lesser bushes that slowly leads me there. Only after my dues are paid will nature lavish her sweetest, biggest, ripest fruit on me.

	FRI.	SAT.	SUN.	MON.
	11	12	13	14

Back home, I try to enforce the same discipline on the family. "Nobody touches these berries," I say, even as they start to disappear to the kids' eager fingers. Finally I have to chase these scavengers away, for the picking on Berry Day is always for the freezer. I spread the berries out on trays in the freezer and, when they're frozen hard, put them into plastic freezer bags. That way they stay separate and, if thawed gently, are pretty close to fresh fruit. We use them throughout the fall and winter in baking, as syrup over ice cream, in fruit compotes or mixed with sparkling water for an incredibly delicious raspberry soda.

Toward the end of The Period of Lesser Heat, the wineberries ripen. Many people call these red raspberries, but they're juicier and sweeter than real red raspberries. Originally from China, wineberries escaped

TUES.	WED.	THURS.	FRI.	
15	16	17	18	

in the eastern U.S. and now are ubiquitous. Although thorny, they aren't as sharp as black raspberries. I can find them in partial shade, especially in eastern and northern exposures. When bright red, they're not quite ripe. It's when they're dark red that their sweetness and flavor peak. They're tender berries and have a slightly waxy feel. Stinkbugs and a long green bug whose name I don't know often feed on them, so one has to look carefully before putting the berries in the mouth. A mother lode of these berries can fill a gallon pail in a half hour—but they're a much sought-after fruit, and I always have competition trying to get to the bushes first.

The blackberries come last and are the trickiest. It's easy enough to insert the arm into the black-berry thicket to reach the ripe berries, but difficult to withdraw it, since the thorns point backward on the stems. Blackberry thorns are the hardest, sharpest and most painful of all the berry bushes, to be approached with caution. Picking is complicated by the fact that not all berries that are black are ripe. The secret is to take only those berries that fall easily into the hand when gently touched by the fingers. The sweetest berries grow in the dry hilltop and moun-tain areas.

Mayapples, blueberries, and huckleberries are yet to come, but since none have thorns, they're easy picking and not in the same class with the wild brambles. It's the brambles that lure me to the hedge-rows and bushes on hot summer days.

In response to the heavy sun, the earth grows a flush of luscious fruit that's celebrated in the picking and celebrated again all winter in the eating. No other seasonal celebration is quite as sweet and beneficent as the ceremony of berry picking and the sacrament of a raspberry tart.

	SAT.	SUN.
	19	20

The Berries

There was an old woman
   Went blackberry picking
Along the hedges
   From Weep to Wicking.
Half a pottle —
   No more she had got,
When out steps a Fairy
   From her green grot;
And says, "Well, Jill,
   Would'ee pick'ee mo?"

And Jill, she curtseys,
   And looks just so.
"Be off," says the Fairy,
   "As quick as you can,
Over the meadows
   To the little green lane,
That dips to the hayfields
   Of Farmer Grimes:
I've berried those hedges
   A score of times;
Bushel on bushel
   I'll promise'ee, Jill,
This side of supper
   If'ee pick with a will."
She glints very bright,
   And speaks her fair;
Then lo, and behold!
   She had faded in air.

Be sure Old Goodie
   She trots betimes
Over the meadows
   To Farmer Grimes.
And never was queen
   With jewelry rich
As those same hedges
   From twig to ditch;

Like Dutchmen's coffers,
   Fruit, thorn, and flower —
They shone like William
   And Mary's Bower.
And be sure Old Goodie
   Went back to Weep,
So tired with her basket
   She scarce could creep.

When she comes in the dusk
   To her cottage door,
There's Towser wagging
   As never before,
To see his Missus
   So glad to be
Come from her fruit-picking
   Back to he.
As soon as next morning
   Dawn was gray,
The pot on the hob
   Was simmering away;
And all in a stew
   And a hugger-mugger
Towser and Jill
   A-boiling of sugar,
And the dark clear fruit
   That from Faerie came
For syrup and jelly
   And blackberry jam.

Twelve jolly gallipots
   Jill put by;
And one little teeny one,
   One inch high;
And that she's hidden
   A good thumb deep,
Half way over
   From Wicking to Weep.

Walter de la Mare

84

Dream Vacation

Suddenly and awkwardly, you're free of the day-to-day routine. The kids go to camp or to Aunt Mabel's. The garden is abandoned for a couple of weeks. Burdens and responsibilities are swung down off the back for a bit. The world's at its hottest, the water's just right for swimming, the big summer moons are going to waste out over the hill. It's time to get out there and have fun.

TA SHU
The Period of Greater Heat

安

July 21–August 4, 1986

The period begins on Monday, July 21, 1986, at 5:41 A.M., at the full moon.

86

The daily routine, for all its predictability and stability, drains us bit by bit over the weeks and months. The same button is pushed day in and day out. Vacation gives us a chance to get some of our other buttons pushed, to make us feel alive. The best vacations are the ones that refresh us the most. Like a good night's sleep.

To sleep; perchance to dream. The body rests in sleep, but the mind doesn't—it dreams. It visits other worlds and strange places in the night. We see and do things we've never done before. Perhaps our dreams suggest to us how to take a real vacation. Now that I think back on past vacations and trips to faraway places, they do seem like dreams to me.

The vacation isn't refreshing because the body gets to rest. It does that for one-third of every day. The refreshment comes from confronting the strange, the

July 21–Aug. 4, 1986

MON.	TUES.	WED.	THURS.	
21	22	23	24	

new and different. Having to deal with new and even intimidating situations forces us to abandon our routine ways of thinking and doing, to get out of our ruts and to walk like careful stalkers over new ground.

Then we are open to learn, to see things in new perspectives, to put things together in new combinations, and to grow. Who can grow when the iron-clad practicalities of everyday life make new thoughts so difficult to apply? The challenge of a good vacation is to forget the everyday rules and make up new ones appropriate to the new situation. This hones our wit and our aptitudes. It sharpens our eye. It makes us aware of everything around us because in new situations, the unexpected can come from any direction. If you have no blind side, you're not likely to get blind-sided.

A good vacation, then, opens our awareness and quickens us. When we return to daily routines, we can see the rut for what it is. We have the perspective to leap over the rut, to create new ways of being, to improve, to find more time for the things closest to our hearts. When we return to our gardens, for instance, they will have had a chance to grow quietly, without

	FRI.	SAT.	SUN.	MON.
	25	26	27	28

our fussing over them. They will certainly have new weeds but, more important, they'll have corners where the flowers or vegetables filled in and made spots of unexpected beauty.

Let's celebrate the liberating vacation. Better still, let's take one.

⊷ The Ocean ⊷

People flock to the shores of America at this time of year. Sure, it's cool and breezy at the shore. Sure, the shore dinners are flapping fresh. But more fundamentally, people return to dip their bodies in the cool, constant mother of us all—the sea.

Scientists say that the concentration of salt in our blood reflects the amount in sea water when the first animals crept onto the shores. They carried some of the ocean with them in their blood, and the seas still thunder within us. We are mostly water, and the moon pulls on us, too.

Immersed in sea water, we are home. The rapture of the deep sings to us through all our years that the sea is a salty symphony, that she is the healer, and that eventually the water in our bodies will find its way home to her.

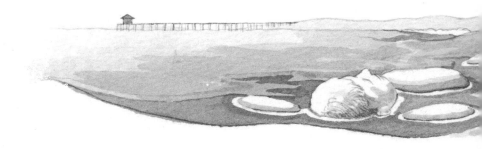

TUES.	WED.	THURS.	FRI.	
29	30	31	1	

Summer Sun

Great is the sun, and wide he goes
Through empty heaven without repose;
And in the blue and glowing days
More thick than rain he showers his rays.

Though closer still the blinds we pull
To keep the shady parlor cool,
Yet he will find a chink or two
To slip his golden fingers through.

The dusty attic, spider-clad,
He, through the keyhole, maketh glad;
And through the broken edge of tiles
Into the laddered hay-loft smiles.

Meantime his golden face around
He bares to all the garden ground,
And sheds a warm and glittering look
Among the ivy's inmost nook.

Above the hills, along the blue,
Round the bright air with footing true,
To please the child, to paint the rose,
The gardener of the World, he goes.

Robert Louis Stevenson

8

9

	SAT.	SUN.	MON.
	2	3	4

Dog Days

Once I chose the Dog Days of August to visit a friend in the Ozark Mountains of Arkansas. The temperature was about 101 and the humidity the same. He lived in a basement that he'd roofed over until the house got built, but he's 15 years into the place and has never built the house. He made his accommodations — now he boasts that his place has a drain in every room.

LI CHHIU
*The Period of
Beginning of Autumn* 火

August 5–August 18, 1986

The period begins on Tuesday, August 5, 1986, at 1:36 P.M., at the new moon.

The oppressive heat made me sweat sitting still. The Ozark soil is mostly red dust and rock, and hot breezes kicked up dust that stuck to wet skin. I'd arrived after a few days of traveling, and needed a shower to begin with. Now I watched the sweat rivulets make grimy trails down my chest and stomach. He had no indoor plumbing, but there was a stream down in the gulley, and he said that a quarter mile down the stream was a waterfall.

The stream had dried to a light trickle. As I made my way down the gulley, I wondered if the waterfall would be running at all. Picking my way along the stones and through overhanging brush, I noticed movement along the gulley sides. I stopped and my eyes found several camouflaged snakes. They were beautiful creatures who watched me watching them. I bid them good-day and made my way to the falls, spying a few more on the way.

Aug. 5–18, 1986

TUES.	WED.	THURS.	FRI.	
5	6	7	8	

90

The waterfall was low, but it was running about as hard as a regular shower. I had no soap, so I rubbed myself lightly with wet sand. That didn't work very well. Then I saw that leaves of many different plants hung near the waterfall just within reach. I got the notion to rub myself with leaves in lieu of soap. Would any be poisonous, like poison ivy? I didn't know the plants of Arkansas very well and most of the leaves were strange to me. I decided to pick the ones that "looked right" for a body rub and took about a dozen leaves from four or five shrubs. I wet them under the water and tore them up with my hands, then rubbed them all over myself. Then I went back under the water for a final rinse.

As I dried out on a big rock in the stream bed, I saw more snakes. I'd never seen any like these, their colors and markings varied like dappled sunlight. They seemed oblivious to me. Were any poisonous, like the copperheads at home? So what if they were? I had no intention of bothering them.

Cooled off and completely refreshed—and smelling like the forest—I put on fresh clothes and started back. The climb was all uphill and by the time I reached the house, I was sweating again. The wind came and kicked dust in my eyes and over my sweaty skin. Within minutes I was as dirty as I was before I bathed. I learned that in the Ozarks, one gives in to dirt and heat and sweat. At least during the Dog Days.

	SAT.	SUN.	MON.	TUES.
	9	10	11	12

The sweltering heat of the Dog Days reminds us to accept the things we can't change. When all our energy is used to fight and deny the inevitable, we don't have much left for clever accommodation.

∽ Microbes ∽

If the summer solstice was the high noon of the year, now it's getting on in the afternoon. The mad rush of growth in the garden has slowed and almost stopped. Leaves have been hanging for months, giving fungi and molds a chance to grab a toehold. Now the hot, muggy weather provides just the right conditions for an explosion of all kinds of decay organisms and infectious germs.

Swimming water had better be clean at this time of year. Cuts fester if not cared for. Infections are harder to conquer. The foliage and herbiage in backyards, fields, and forests become dotted and chewed. Tomatoes ripen and rot in one day if not kept off the ground.

If we could have microscopic eyes and peer into the smaller world just out of range of our vision, we would see the most furious activity everywhere: fungi, molds, and bacteria building structures, attacking everything, running wild in the ripe, hot, moist world. Their function in the world is all-important, for they dismantle the used-up, discarded, and weak structures that life has put together. Without them, the world would be clogged with the dead shells of creatures past. The microbes recycle nutrients to young plants, which support all animal life.

This is their time of the year to shine. Let's recognize their contribution to nature's cycles by making a compost pile that sets a *real* feast before them.

WED.	THURS.	FRI.	SAT.	
13	14	15	16	

❧ Frosty Thoughts ❧

Now I'm glad I took the time to store away some frosty thoughts and images last January.

On some bitter cold January day, when the sassafras has crystalline ice on its fingertips and the snow drifts around its boles, I find myself thinking, "If I can just absorb this scene, this feeling of ice and cold, and lock it away in my mind, maybe I can use it to cool off on some hot summer day." And so I pretend my head is a videocassette recorder and my eyes are the camera, and I pan across the frozen wastes of my property, cut to two crows cawing their way west under the gray sky, then to a close-up of a stalk of dried Queen Anne's lace supporting a puff of white snow on its umbel.

Dog Days are the perfect time to play back the January images and remember the deliciously cold feelings—how the air was so lightly stinging and transparent. It helps. Of course, now's also the time to store away some images of sweltering heat to enjoy on a frosty winter's day.

	SUN.	MON.
	17	18

❧ Corn City ❧

The Indians were not wrong in thinking of corn as God's gift to mankind. One way to celebrate the gift is with a corn bake: Dig a pit 18 inches deep and 18 inches wide, and make it as long as you need for the corn you'll roast. Early in the morning, build a wood fire in the length of the pit and burn it all day. Late in the afternoon, smooth out the coals and throw on several layers of wet burlap. Then lay the corn, still in its husks, on the burlap and cover with more wet burlap. Cover this with cornstalks and husks and let it bake for an hour or so.

❧ A Hint of Fall ❧

The weather can remain beastly hot but something changes ever so slightly during this period. Perhaps it's the first fungus-spotted black walnut leaves that drift into the driveway. Or it could be a barely perceptible diminution of the sun's intensity. But the Chinese name for this time, Beginning of Autumn, is right on target. It's still weeks from autumn, but a process has begun that won't be stopped until summer slips off the edge of the world at the fall equinox.

Gathering of Birds

This is a joyous time for the birds. The sun is warm, but the edge is off the intense heat. The fields are full of seeds and grains and the fruit is on the vine. The nestlings are flown, and breeding pairs split up.

CHHU SHU
*The Period of
End of Heat* 天

August 19–September 3, 1986

The period begins on Tuesday, August 19, 1986, at 1:54 P.M., at the full moon.

It's not time to make the long journey south for the winter, so nature has the birds on vacation.

With little to do and plenty to eat, the birds start to congregate. Small groups form, which aggregate later into flocks. They'll go on feeding forays or hang out in a tree playing hopscotch on the branches. They remind me of a group of human friends at a resort: boisterous, silly, flying around just for the hell of it. I've seen a bird at this time of year stand straight up and walk a branch like a drunk on a white line. The territorial squabbles are over, and the birds are having fun, putting on weight, storing energy for the migration's great exertion.

With the gathering of birds, nature begins to draw up the first strings of summer. These little groups are brought together by a secret affinity that will lead them safely through a coming winter. In this season when the birds gather, let's celebrate their quick, easy response to their secret affinity and pray that ours might be as true.

Aug. 19–Sept. 3, 1986

TUES.	WED.	THURS.	FRI.	
19	20	21	22	

When a Watermelon Is Ripe. . .

Watermelons are plump in the patch now. There are three rules of thumb to tell when a watermelon is ripe:

It Makes a Hollow Sound. Knock on the melon; it should sound hollow, not dull.

The Underside Turns Yellow. Look at the spot that's been on the ground. It should be turning yellow.

The Stem Withers. Even if the stem doesn't come loose from the melon, the melon may be ripe if the stem is turning dry.

SAT.	SUN.	MON.	TUES.
23	24	25	26

≋ Labor Day ≋

The Period of End of Heat usually includes Labor Day, after which schools reopen and summer's carefree attitude gives way to one of knuckling down and getting back to earnest work.

The precious days leading up to Labor Day are among the finest in the year. The earth is quiet and still, in the last stages of ripening. The sun's heat is diminished and the nights are cool. It's a great time for parties and a last fling at the summer sports. The last trip to the beach is poignant as the slow evening comes and lingers over the water. Everyone can feel something begin to slip away.

The work of spring and summer is coming to fruition in the garden. We can relax now as everything gets ready for the big harvest. Family dinners feature late corn and lots of ripe tomatoes. For most of us, the garden is our only chance to get a quick and direct

WED.	THURS.	FRI.	SAT.	
27	28	29	30	

payoff from our work. We invest a few hours in May and June and we enjoy the incomparable garden-fresh flavors of homegrown food in late August. Let the world's economies fluctuate! Price an apple at a dime or a dollar, what does the gardener care? The price of his apple is an hour spent at pruning and another spent at cluster thinning. An apple is always worth an apple to the person who grew it.

Too bad that modern life so many times removes us from the results of our work. No wonder that so many good people work at jobs that cause mischief—they never get to see or assess the results of their effort in the natural world.

The garden shows us that we get out what we put in—but with great increase made possible by the bountiful disposition of nature. This Labor Day, let's celebrate our working relationship with our gardens by inviting just our homegrown produce to dinner.

	SUN.	MON.	TUES.	WED.
	31	1	2	3

∽ Campfire ∽

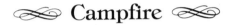

If you don't have a hearth for a campfire in your
yard, make one now, for the campfire days are on us.
Maybe we take a hint from the gathering birds, but
the most satisfying thing in the world becomes to sit
around the campfire at night, staring into the flames
and telling stories about the fast-fading summer.

The nights are perfect: cool, full of stars, filled
with the chugging of crickets and katydids. The glow
of the campfire lights up the faces sitting around it.
The ancient archetypal ring appears, where talk is the
medium and the game is to spot truth as it ripples
through.

This campfire talk is not the hyper, reach-a-goal
speech of midday. The flames fill the spaces between
the carefully considered words. Silence enters into the
conversation. Ideas aren't backed up in everyone's
minds, waiting impatiently to come out. People can
really listen. Nothing's invested in a conversation that
is dominated by the flames of a campfire, except that
the sounds of speech and flames enact a ritual as old
as mankind itself.

MAKE A SKYHOOK

In this season of summer-ending flings and get-togethers, you'll need a skyhook to entertain the kids (and any adults who've never seen one). With this simple shape and a leather belt, you can seemingly defy gravity.

Make the skyhook this size and in this shape from a thin piece of wood or <u>very</u> stiff cardboard.

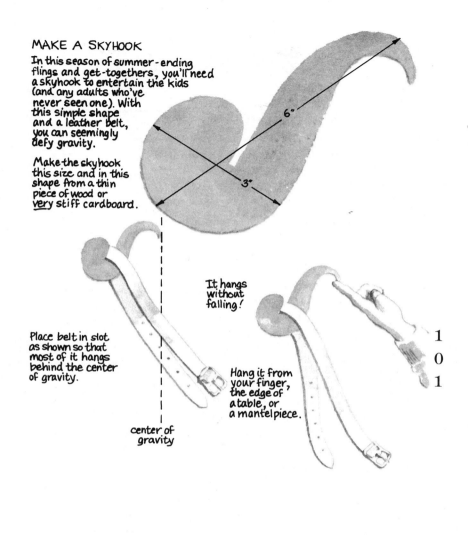

6"

3"

It hangs without falling!

Place belt in slot as shown so that most of it hangs behind the center of gravity.

center of gravity

Hang it from your finger, the edge of a table, or a mantelpiece.

Country Fair

There are always gardeners who consistently take prizes at the country fairs. And some gardeners think bigger than that. They go for world-record vegetables.

There's money in big vegetables if they're successful. The Half Moon Bay Pumpkin Festival in San Francisco has been offering $10,000 to anyone who brings in a world-record pumpkin. The *Guinness Book of World Records* is used as the official standard; at this writing it lists a Nova Scotia grower's 493.5 pound behemoth. The New Jersey Tomato Weigh-In offers $1,000 for the biggest tomato grown in the state each year. A recent first-prize winner weighed in at 3.53 pounds. While big, it's far short of the world-record 6.5-pound tomato grown in Monona, Wisconsin, in 1977.

How do the winners do it? A few years ago the Associated Press carried the story of a Mexican farmer who grew giant vegetables—onions as big around as bushel baskets and cabbages that fit three to a pickup truck. *Organic Gardening* sent an investigative reporter there to check out the story. He returned in a few weeks having seen no actual giant vegetables, but he did acquire some photos.

PAI LU
The Period of White Dews

大

September 4–September 22, 1986

The period begins on Thursday, September 4, 1986, at 2:10 A.M., at the new moon. It includes the full moon on Thursday, September 18, 1986, at 12:34 A.M.

1
0
2

Sept. 4–22, 1986

THURS.	FRI.	SAT.	SUN.	
4	5	6	7	

They seemed to be legitimate snapshots of big
onions and other vegetables, but one was a postcard of
a truck groaning under the load of two cabbages. On
the back of the postcard it said, "The Fabulous Giant
Vegetables of the Valley." We grew suspicious.

The reporter had interviewed the farmer, who
claimed that spacemen from the Pleiades bearing a
set of secret instructions for growing giant vegetables
had imparted this knowledge to him. We killed the
story.

You don't need a Martian map to grow big
vegetables. The rules include proper shading and
plenty of water and fertilizer. It's important to start
with a variety of seed known to produce large fruit
(such as the Big Max pumpkin). Only one fruit, ear,
head, or edible part should be allowed to grow on each
plant, in order to concentrate the grow-power into that
specimen.

MON.	TUES.	WED.	THURS.	FRI.
8	9	10	11	12

The only technique shared by every grower of prize-winning vegetables is to give the plants lots of tender loving care. That means weeding and mulching and hand-picking insects. It means coaxing your plant to grow big. There's a story about Luther Burbank that has him talking to a cactus plant, urging it to produce a seedling with no thorns. Burbank promised the plant that he wouldn't allow it to be harmed if it dropped its thorns. In the next generation, there appeared a thornless type that's supplied the genes for many of today's thornless cacti. That kind of relationship is a part of growing giant vegetables. The final requirement is a giant green thumb.

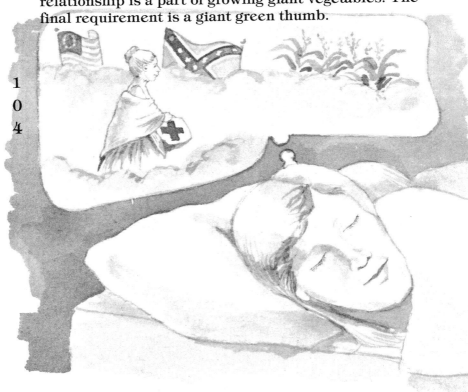

SAT.	SUN.	MON.	TUES.	WED.	
13	14	15	16	17	

≋ Sleeping Weather ≋

Here's something to celebrate: The nights are cool enough for the comforter. Bed seems just the place to be on the cool end of a warm September day. It's not yet time to crank up the wood stove, but it's time for getting snug.

And for the kind of vivid, technicolor dreams in which you find yourself looking at the ridgetops protruding above the morning mist. You're walking along a dusty path into the rising sun. You hear the crash of muskets beyond the cornfield on your left and the boom of cannon batteries firing to your right. A rolling wall of smoke is speeding toward you and in it, swirling just below the surface of the smoke, are the flags and the faces of the men carried off in the maelstrom of the Civil War . . .

And for the kind of dream you don't recall exactly, except that it was something important to remember when you woke up.

And for the dreams of childhood, confined again to schoolrooms and hallways, lunchrooms and lavatories, while outside the September sun dazzles the eyes through the windows.

Tonight, let's get into bed early. That's always a great way to line up some *good* dreams.

THURS.	FRI.	SAT.	SUN.	MON.
18	19	20	21	22

Middle Age

All the experiences of childhood and the growth and flowering of young adulthood are over. Now's the time to slowly ripen the fruit. When they're young, it's hard to tell which plants or people will bear the best fruit. Sometimes it's the inconspicuous broccoli in the back of the patch that matures the perfect head.

CHUI FEN
*The Period of
Autumn Equinox* 活

September 23–October 2, 1986

The period begins on Tuesday, September 23, 1986, at 2:59 A.M., at the autumn equinox.

Ripening is a more internal process than growth and flowering in the sense that great uptake of nutrients and inputs isn't required. In many plants, the leaves, stems, and stalks will turn brown and wither away before the fruit is ripe. Ground-cherries, for instance, taste sweetest after the first frosts—a posthumous tribute to the plant that bore them.

To the young, middle age may look undesirable. Physical prowess lessens. The body needs help from glasses and false teeth. The trend no longer plunges onward and upward, but slides slowly down toward death.

But while youth may have more sheer energy, it tends to be dissipated in many directions, wasted, squandered on what later are seen to be inconsequential gratifications. In middle age, one knows what one's talents are. The lessened vigor is still more than enough to achieve the miraculous when it is focused and intensified on tasks to which the person brings a

Sept. 23–Oct. 2, 1986

TUES.	WED.	THURS.	FRI.	
23	24	25	26	

lifetime of experience. In fact, the energy that a middle-aged person can bring to bear on a task is usually far more concentrated, practiced, and artful than that of youth. Boredom is no longer a possibility. The prospect is not one of slow decline toward death at all, but a continually refined and richer work, trimmed of excess in order to achieve completion before death.

Middle age, like the time of ripening for plants, is when a person gets to enjoy the long sunny days of early autumn, to feel the integration of life's lessons and experiences into qualities like wisdom, discipline, and understanding—qualities that suffuse the person expressing them with quiet joy.

Let youth enjoy its struggle up the cliff-face of life. In middle age, the top has already been gained and the vistas are vast and fresh. One is simultaneously at the peak of one's powers and able to relax the struggle to become. The middle-aged have already become what they truly are, and if what they are is beautiful, their work will show it.

	SAT.	SUN.	MON.	TUES.
	27	28	29	30

The little green and swelling apple may be cute. It may be promising. It may even be unblemished and perfect. But only the ripe apple hanging ready to pick, blushed with glowing colors, is beautiful.

As the autumn equinox signifies the boundary between summer's light and winter's darkness, so middle age signifies a turning point in life. But whatever is taken away from creatures in later life is replaced in great measure by finer stuff. While an older person may not be able to run a foot race with the kids, she can remember running such races and understand the children and their fun. This understanding brings deep appreciation of the kids and their bursting life. Heightened appreciation then brings a heightened enjoyment of life.

As the ripe apple is most enjoyable, so the ripened life is most enjoyable. Middle age, at last, is what it's all for.

⚜ Fishing ⚜

The nights are cooling off now and the water in creeks and lakes is getting colder. The fish are stirring from their summer torpor and beginning to rise near the shore.

Every fisherman dreams of places where the fish will surely bite. He may never have seen the spot, but always in his dreams the fish are rising. Many dreams are better left as fantasy, but one year I brought a fishing dream to life by spending a few days at a remote lake in wilderness Maine. From the shore, I could hear only two red squirrels chittering in the pines—not a car, not an airplane, not a whisper. The silence was palpable.

WED.	THURS.
1	2

The boat bumping into the water and the water's slap and burble on its sides broke the heavy stillness, and then I was drifting free into the deeper parts. The surface of the lake seemed so placid—could there be any fish there at all?

To my right, I saw the water roil. Fish were rising! I started the engine and gave it a burst of speed, then shut it off and drifted quietly toward the troubled water. By the time I got there, the fish were gone. So I fished my way back to deeper water, then back toward the boat landing. No nibbles in two hours; I thought about taking a hike, then fishing in the evening, when they'd be biting. No sooner had I made the decision to quit fishing than a 12-inch native trout took my wet fly. Soon she was in the boat. I was so grateful. Grateful that she'd bit. Grateful that she didn't get away. Grateful that I'd get to taste a real native Maine trout.

She was more than I'd imagined—pink, sweet flesh perfectly cooked. Although the portion was skimpy, each bite was a dream come true.

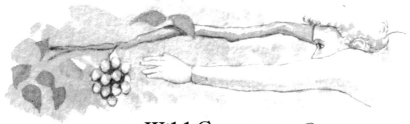

❧ Wild Grapes ❧

We moved from the densely packed suburbs of Long Island to a country place deep in Pennsylvania's Pocono Mountains when I was 10. The transition was difficult, but I see in retrospect that the move had some extraordinary benefits, chiefly that I was old enough to know what was going on when I discovered country life. I never knew there were wild grapes, for example, except maybe they had something to do with Leif Ericsson in a storybook. But during the September after we moved, my friend and I were walking down a dirt road when I smelled the most delicious, fruity aroma. The road was lined with sassafras trees, and high in their branches hung bunches of grapes, black against the pale yellow-green of the undersides of sassafras and grape leaves. The smell was a mixture of fruit gum and Welch's grape juice, a perfume concocted expressly for the 11-year-old sensibility. There was no question but that we were going to get those grapes.

We shinnied and grunted up the slim trunks and stood among the flimsy branches. The smell and the bunches of big, black, wild grapes were all around us. I tasted my first wild grape berry. Can I truthfully remember that first taste? Absolutely. Wild grapes still taste the same. It's just that none will ever again surprise me with its foxy, wild flavor the way that the first grape did on my perch 15 feet up and several decades ago.

The bear puts both arms around the tree above her
And draws it down as if it were a lover
And its choke-cherries lips to kiss goodbye,
Then lets it snap back upright in the sky.

Robert Frost

∞ Crossing the Equator ∞

Navies have a tradition of hazing sailors—no matter what their rank—when they first cross the equator. Now the sun crosses the equator and will smile on the Southern Hemisphere for six long months. From this period on, the sun will be noticeably weaker, its heat subsiding and its light thinner. The late September haze that whitens our mornings may be the sun's farewell to us, its hazing at crossing the equator, the trail of summer's heat now obscured by a cool dew.

Harvests

"You reap what you sow" doesn't quite do justice to the process. "You reap a thousand times more than you sow" is more like it. Compare the tomato seed to the total foliage and fruit it will produce in a good spot and it may be that we reap a million times more. Not only will a garden produce a year's worth of vegetables from a handful of seed but its fertility and grow-power will *increase* over a season when handled organically.

Now's the time when everything is ready to pick and store away for the coming winter. Potatoes in boxes fill the root cellar. Butternut squashes replace the old shoes on the floor of a cool upstairs closet. The carrots will be thickly mulched and stay in their garden beds. Beets are pickled. Belgian endive roots are dug up, trimmed, and buried in boxes. Apples are cut into slices and dried on strings. Grapes tumble through the juice press. Nuts are falling like hail from the big wild nut trees—hickory, butternut, walnut, and beech. You've sowed some of this harvest yourself, but much more just bursts forth from a bountiful earth.

There's a lot of repetitive handwork to the harvest season. Thousands of turns on the tomato juicer. Thousands of apple slices. Little assembly lines running here and there in the harvest kitchen fill the cabinets and shelves with richly colored jars of

---

HAN LU
The Period of Cold Dews

October 3–October 16, 1986

The period begins on Friday, October 3, 1986, at 1:55 P.M., at the new moon.

112

Oct. 3–16, 1986

FRI.	SAT.	SUN.	MON.	
3	4	5	6	

homegrown food. Outside, the yellow jackets and hornets gorge on the sugar splashing out of all the ripe fruit. With the kitchen a soggy mess, celebrate the harvest by going out to dinner tonight.

❧ The Blue Balmies ❧

In this period, we're usually treated to spells of perfect weather. The days begin cool and misty. The sun eventually burns the fog away, revealing cobalt-blue skies. Many plants are still green but many others have finished their summer seeding and are brown and drying. Pools of deep red begin to spread on the blackberry leaves. It's warm in the sunlight, but chill lurks in the shadows. By midafternoon the air has warmed enough to feel comfortable everywhere, but this doesn't last as the sun descends. By nightfall there's a sharp cold that seeps right up to the edges of a campfire. High above in the cold crystal air, the stars look more brilliant and clear, reminding you of winter nights when they're out to stare you down. By 2 A.M. it's very cold.

These are work days: building, working wood, making soft and subtle wreaths from dried wayside plants. It's time to rearrange the tool shed. And to open the house to the cool, clean air, allowing its

	TUES.	WED.	THURS.	FRI.
	7	8	9	10

dryness to pull summer's sticky moisture from the furniture, rugs, and beds. This is weather to hew and split logs for winter's fires.

Perhaps most of all, it's weather to walk out on the hill and sit among the foliage beginning to marshal its colors. Look over the fading remnants of summer and then out across the miles. The earth has much to tell us at this point—about summing up, about what's important.

 Golf

The Blue Balmies are perfect weather for golfing, so if you're going to go, let me give you a tip. The little white ball with the dimples in it is extremely dangerous. It is a potent totem that draws forth whatever anger, frustration, and rage have been stored in the golfer since his last outing. Lest the potent totem draw forth *your* rage and tears, I suggest you play without one. Players who burn in agony over bad shots, triple bogeys, and diabolical lies are simply using the course as a personal purgatory. For you, it'll be heaven. Just forget the ball.

1
1
4

SAT.	SUN.	MON.	TUES.	
11	12	13	14	

❧ Apple Cider ❧

At one time, apple cider was the national drink of America. Although it's long since been replaced by cola, it remains exquisite, natural, and thirst-quenching. We're not talking about the apple juice you buy in stores, which is generally reconstituted from apple concentrate and tastes like sweet-and-sour water. Apple cider, at its best, is bought at the mill and is a heady, perfumy mixture of the juice of several different apples and strains of fruit flies.

We once put up 120 quarts of apple cider. After picking a pickup-truckful of apples, we drove to the upper floor of our local cider mill on a road that curls up around back. The apples are dumped onto a conveyor belt, which drops them into a pulper. Inside the mill, the pulp falls onto a tarpaulin lying on the press. When enough pulp is on the sheet, the edges are folded over and another sheet is laid on top. When five such sheets are stacked, the framework is moved under the press and a wooden platform placed on top of the stack. Then the press descends and slowly squeezes out the juice, which runs down a trough into a holding tank on the second floor. This tank has hoses to a first-floor filling room, where we filled six 5-gallon carboys with fresh cider.

At home we built a large wood fire outside and borrowed 5-gallon pots to boil the cider in. Boiled Mason jars were filled with the hot cider and sealed.

Later in the season, when we opened them, the juice still tasted fresh and delicious, with an added light smoky taste from the wood fire. The perfect drink to celebrate the harvest and the advancing autumn.

	WED.	THURS.
	15	16

Color Fiesta

The line crosses into the United States from Canada in September and creeps steadily south. By this period, it has crossed Pennsylvania and exploded throughout Appalachia. Behind the line, the leaves of the eastern hardwood trees speckle with color, increasing in intensity until the world is finally aflame with harmonized reds, yellows, burgundies, and golds.

My teachers always claimed that the colors were in the leaves to begin with. We couldn't see them because they were drowned out by the dominating green of living chlorophyll. Although I've never had reason to doubt this, I've never wholeheartedly believed it, either. They'd explain that after the first frosts, trees seal off the places where leaf stems join the branches. Neither water nor nutrients can reach the leaves, nor can any more manufactured sugars be sent down into the tree. The chlorophyll disintegrates and the reds and yellows of cyanic compounds emerge. While logical, the scientific explanation seemed to me to miss the point.

As if she has saved the best for last, nature arranges for the growing season to end in a blaze of glory. A last hurrah. The grand finale of her chromatic pyrotechnics. Are such colors just an artifact of leaf

SHUANG CHIANG
The Period of
Descent of Frost 化

October 17–November 1, 1986

The period begins on Friday, October 17, 1986, at 2:22 P.M., at the full moon.

Oct. 17–Nov. 1, 1986

	FRI.	SAT.	SUN.	MON.	
	17	18	19	20	

senescence, or are they farewell-party decorations for earth's green spirits? It's the poetic vision, after all, that gives science a context.

I have walked on late October afternoons among these colors and become drunk with them. Careful attention reveals effortless color harmonies that the greatest artists have to struggle to approximate. There was a bush along our driveway whose leaves a few autumns ago were a light yellow-green. Because the leaves were dying, a fungus covered them with evenly spaced chocolate-brown dots. Glowing silently in the warm October light, this ordinary bush was a fantasy from a fable. Ten feet away, red maple leaf stars poured over golden hickory fronds. Soft yellow leaves from a tall tulip poplar carpeted the ground below the livid purples and reds of a sassafras. I remember

	TUES.	WED.	THURS.	FRI.
	21	22	23	24

having to sit down to drink it in. Here was a brocade made with a skill beyond human hands, and I was woven into it, laced with color, drunk with color.

The forest slowly blazes up to a fiery crescendo, then dies quickly to embers speckling the black and gray of the winter forest. And then even these last bits of color flutter down and turn dun brown on the ground. Color leaves the earth and rushes to the western sky.

That's it. The growing season's over. Icy teeth form on the driveway's puddles at night. All that's left is the winter sunset, a memory of the blazing woods.

❧ First Frosts ❧

For most of the U.S., The Period of Descent of Frost is aptly named. In the higher western elevations and the very northern parts of the country, frosts have been occurring for a month. But across much of the vast heartland and east, school kids break open thin slices of ice from puddles and scuffle in the white hoarfrost on the green grass.

Now you can tell the native North American plants from European colonizers. Native North American plants know what's in store—the furious winters, the winds at 10 below zero. They check out and turn brown with the first frosts. European colonizers, however, still believe they're in Brittany, where the winters are cloudy, wet, and not much more severe than Georgia's. You'll notice that wild grasses are brown and beige. Lawn grasses—originally European types—are green and still going for it. Native sugar maples have gone off like skyrockets and dropped their leaves, while imported Norway maples hang on to their leaves as if winter were going to be a passing cold spell.

SAT.	SUN.	MON.	TUES.	
25	26	27	28	

For most green growing tissue, however, frost forms ice within cells and bursts them open. Death is dancing heavy on the earth at this time. Halloween images are gruesome and appropriate. At this season of human life, too, death is a more frequent visitor. If hearty laughter is a sign of a courageous attitude in life, it is doubly that when confronting death's feathery fingers on the window panes. Therefore do the Germans cavort at Oktoberfest and the Americans at Halloween. This is a season of merry parties. While the world dies around us, let's celebrate with a bash.

	WED.	THURS.	FRI.	SAT.
	29	30	31	1

This paper airplane won a
contest several years ago. It's
an ingenious design perfect for
lofting during a study hall in high school.
How can the study hall teacher possibly find
fault with the aerodynamic genius who launches
one of these?

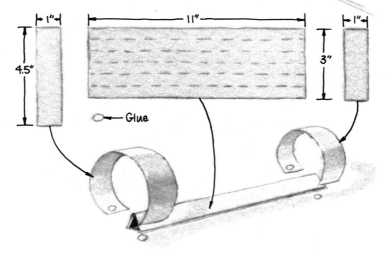

1
2
0

1"   11"   1"

4.5"   3"

Glue

❧ Indian Summer ❧

Sometime in late October or early November, mild weather returns. The days are lazy, hazy, smoky, and quiet. The sun seems to regain some power and survivors of the first frosts are rewarded with summer's reprise. But it is not summer. She's merely another ghost dancing in the smoke that hangs over the cornfield.

One can try to recapture something of summer — the fun of a softball game, a run on country roads — but it is not summer that one gets. The soul of summer is flown. The fun is only a reenactment.

Summer is gone and so are the Indians. Summer slain by ruthless advance of winter, the Indians melted away before the disease and disruption of the colonists. Maybe it is because their ghosts linger in the quiet places of the woods and fields that this season is melancholy despite our brave attempts at cheerfulness.

The Winter Place

Coats and sweaters are routine now. Nights dip below freezing. The breath steams. The sun is no longer strong enough to evaporate the morning dew, and the tumbled weeds and grasses stay wet. Down near the ground, the last cricket, large and lumbering, slowly pulls himself over the wet, rotting plants. The leaves are down and old familiar winter vistas open up.

LI TUNG
The Period of Beginning of Winter

November 2–November 14, 1986

The period begins on Sunday, November 2, 1986, at 1:02 A.M., at the new moon.

1
2
2

The winter place returns. The indoors becomes a place to be comfortable and work, rather than a place to stash things while we run outside.

Summer is put away. Lawn furniture is stored, the tools wiped with oil and put in the shed. Hammocks are folded. Leaves blow over the flagstones and collect in the remains of the hosta border. The sun gives light without heat, and again we get used to taking our warmth from the stove.

How easy it is to finally accept the winter place: It's cozy in there. It feels good to sit by the fire—much better than outside. Gives one a chance to catch up on reading or listen to music. Besides, that TV show's on tonight and who feels like going out anyway?

Limitation goes along with survival at this season. We need to forget the green mansions of days gone by and enjoy the quiet room of winter, where everything

Nov. 2–14, 1986

SUN.	MON.	TUES.	WED.	
2	3	4	5	

is within reach, and we know where everything is. It gives us time to take stock.

The walls and cabinets of the winter place are lined with the fruits of our summer work. Each jar carries more than nutrition to the table—it carries memories of summer days and seedlings in the spring. There are more than enough jars to carry us through. More than enough memories to last the rest of a lifetime.

The winter place is, after all, a blessing, for we can no longer live in the wider world at large.

❧ The Geese Go South ❧

The geese close out the season. Their honking signals other birds, for the winter birds are returning. Food is abundant from now until the snows; weeds, Virginia creeper, poison ivy, dogwood, and many other forest and field plants are loaded with high-nourishment seeds. Rich vegetable fats in the fall seeds power the migrating birds on their long journeys. One naturalist theorizes that seeds turn bright colors when ripe to signal their edibility to the birds. The birds in turn disperse the seeds, preserving the plant.

1
2
3

	THURS.	FRI.	SAT.	SUN.
	6	7	8	9

❧ And So to Bed ❧

And so to bed goes the garden. Clean it up now.
Pull and compost the rank weed growth that's dried in
place. Use the deluge of leaves to renew the mulch on
the garden paths. Turn up the soil in the growing beds
and cover it with manure and mulch.

You accomplish several important things with a
fall garden clean-up. Seed pods on the weed stalks
will all surely shatter over winter, throwing down
enough weed seed to keep you in lamb's-quarters for
several centuries. If you've allowed weeds to go to
seed, pulling them now will reduce the number reaching
the ground. Also, insects overwinter in trash and
rotting stalks—refurbishing the beds gets rid of them.
Vegetables left to rot in the ground over winter harbor
fungi you may not want around next growing season.
The nicely prepared beds and mulched walkways look
better over winter than a rank patch that reminds you
of the work you didn't do last August.

By incorporating fresh manure into the soil, then
mulching with spoiled hay, you give winter a chance to
be useful in the garden. Alternate freezes and thaws
begin to break down the manure. Although it's cold,
the manure will rot and partially disintegrate under
mulch that itself is under snow. The mulch will lose
structure and be ready for incorporation into the soil
in the spring. Snow brings a little extra nitrogen.

When spring comes, you're not faced straight off
with a lot of work. The mulched, manured beds are
ready for spinach, onions, peas, and other early crops
as soon as the snow melts. So tuck the garden in,
blow it a goodnight kiss, and wish it pleasant dreams.
It will cheer the November gloom to know you've
taken care of business and are already ready for
spring.

1
2
4

MON.	TUES.	WED.	THURS.	
10	11	12	13	

Envoy

They are not long, the weeping and the laughter,
    Love and desire and hate;
I think they have no portion in us after
    We pass the gate.

They are not long, the days of wine and roses;
    Out of a misty dream
Our path emerges for a while, then closes
    Within a dream.

Ernest Dowson

125

❧ Hunting ❧

Hunting carries us deep into the wild places, to ledges and paths and parts of the forest we've never seen. Although our quarry may be elusive, we always find something worth the hike. It may be a small animal skull or a piece of quartz. It may be the refreshment we get from a small spring far from any source of pollution—a refreshment beyond the bounds of our knowledge. It may be the sight of creamy-yellow willow leaves against the backdrop of the black forest floor, or gelatinous red cups of a fungus sprouting from a tree stump. It may be the hilltop view of a deep valley with woodsmoke curling up from the chimney of a house and the glint of a faraway river. It may be a spot under the toasty-brown leaves of a beech, inviting the hunter to rest against its gray bark. It may be the animals and insects we see unexpectedly. It may be the togetherness with nature that fills us with satisfaction. I found out long ago that a gun is a dangerous and unnecessary prop to take along on such a hunt. Communion with nature is the meat of the soul. And nothing has to die to make the day a success.

Thanksgiving

The growing season is over and the harvest is stored away. Cold intensifies and the last flowers freeze. In the north, snow has already fallen. Farther south, it becomes an imminent possibility.

HSIAO HSÜEH
The Period of Lesser Snow

思

November 15–November 30, 1986

The period begins on Saturday, November 15, 1986, at 7:12 A.M., at the full moon.

This is the time of year to make a summation, to count blessings, and to celebrate the peculiarly American institution of Thanksgiving. Now we give back some of what's been given. One of the benefits of being a gardener is an infinite supply of things to be thankful for.

128

—Thanks for the chance to work the earth through another cycle.

—Thanks for timely rains.

—Thanks for seeds—the sparks that set off a green conflagration in the summer garden.

—Thanks for the smell of basil. And of tomato plants.

—Thanks for blue flowers.

—Thanks for moments of peace and quiet, when the most growing is done.

—Thanks for the taste of dill and the texture of Sugar Snap peas.

—Thanks for kids who love to eat fresh from the garden. May they learn to work in it, too.

Nov. 15–30, 1986

SAT.	SUN.	MON.	TUES.	
15	16	17	18	

—Thanks for the bubblegum colors of the portulaca.
—Thanks for making them male and female.
What an inspired idea!
—Thanks for what happens to dirt when you
manure it.
—Thanks for the transformation of rain water into
sap and juice.
—Thanks for the hidden meanings all through the
garden, and for the values they lead to.
—Thanks especially for birds.
—Thanks for everything.

	WED.	THURS.	FRI.	SAT.
	19	20	21	22

The Fuel on the Hill

I like to split logs by hand with a splitting maul. The object becomes to pop the log apart with one economical blow. Each time a log splits open, I am the first person in the world to see this grain. Heretofore it had been hidden beneath the bark and in the dark interior of the tree. But opened to light, it reveals color, texture, and pattern. Wood is the tree's chief product, and it's crafted with precision along flowing lines. One sees the patterns of rivers in the wood as it courses around knots and limbs and splits to flow around crotches. Wood appears to be a solidified pattern of flowing water, created by the liquids in the tree, produced layer by layer through the years.

Dried but Not Forgotten

Dried summer and fall flowers make magnificent wreaths and arrangements in soft and subtle colors. Here are a few we've used.

Statice: The variety that dries to a deep blue is most common in the garden, although white and pink are sometimes seen.

Pearly Everlasting: This wild flower has a woodsy, pleasant smell and a beautiful pearly look.

Globe Amaranth: A prolific bearer of lavender, white, or orange globes that dry perfectly.

Coxcomb: The intense red wattles add color to an arrangement.

Lamb's Ears: Pick the silvery, woolly flower spikes when they just start to open a few purple flowers. Beautiful in arrangements. It's a garden perennial.

SUN.	MON.	TUES.	WED.	
23	24	25	26	

Wild and Ornamental Grasses: Sprays and seed heads make vivid elements in an arrangement.

Strawflowers: Pick the flower heads when they're just opening, not when fully open. Use florists' wires to make stiff stems. Strawflowers grow well in good garden soil.

Yarrow: Wild yarrow is white or light rose. Cultivated types come in gold, pale yellow, pink, and red.

After picking, the flowers or plants should be hung upside down in a warm, dark, dry spot. They're dry when the stems snap rather than bend.

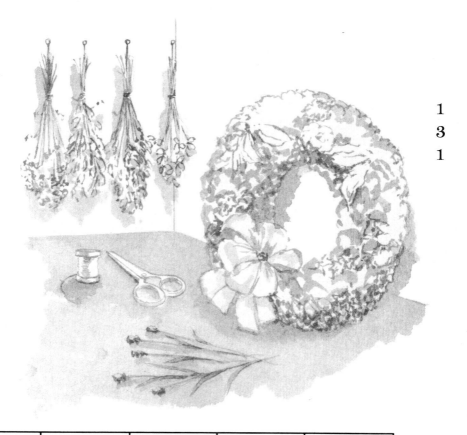

	THURS.	FRI.	SAT.	SUN.
	27	28	29	30

✒ Temporary Retirement ✒

Gardeners retire at this time of year to the kitchen table where, for a while, weeds and watering can be forgotten and other kinds of business can be attended to.

But, of course, the houseplants take a certain amount of care. The windows are filling fast with the winter's crop of philodendron, African violets, hoyas, dracaena, miniature oranges, rabbit's-foot fern, passion flowers, night-blooming jasmine, bougainvillea, and avocado trees. At least, those are some of the flora that live at our house in the winter. Sometimes our upstairs looks like a scene from an "Indiana Jones" movie.

And, of course, I forgot that now the amaryllis comes up from the cellar and the Christmas cactus must be taken up, and bulbs forced . . .

Forget what I said about retirement.

✒ Quietus ✒

The bear and the badger make their quietus now, seeking dens to hunker in while the north winds blow. Nature sends some animals to sleep, stands others on guard. Owls watch the sleeping mounds of snow intently. A rabbit stands upright on moonlit ice and nibbles hips off the wild rose. Deer prune the tips of low shrubs and trees. The songbirds have flown. The air opens up to distant sounds again; it's transparent to sound. From now through winter solstice, the world is quiet and still, waiting for the last sparks to go out so new dreams can form in the deep sleep of the last days of the year.

The Final Days

In my youth, I keenly felt the annual destruction of summer. What a sad sight the world presented at this time of year: devoid of color, dim, leafless, frozen, and wet; utterly ruined.

If I wanted eternal summer, I should have moved to Hollywood. In the temperate zones, one must put up with this annual death, learn to make one's peace with the idea, learn to accept it not only as routine, but also as beneficial.

Death, perversely, is the sweetener of life. Their ephemerality makes the strawberries taste even better. Life's finite span makes every day precious. If we were to live forever in this world, we'd surely feel condemned, for this is not a perfect world. Eternity is an attribute of a perfect world, along with pure truth, beauty, and goodness. On earth, truth tends to be relative, beauty is often marred, and goodness goes begging. The fact that our years and days are numbered in this world forces us to look deeper, see farther, and understand more. And then we perceive the truth among the relationships, use our hands to shape new beauty, and spread goodness though we don't earn a penny or even a word of thanks.

TA HSÜEH
The Period of Greater Snow

完

December 1–December 21, 1986

The period begins on Monday, December 1, 1986, at 11:43 A.M., at the new moon. It includes the full moon on Tuesday, December 16, at 2:04 A.M.

134

Dec. 1–21, 1986

MON.	TUES.	WED.	THURS.	
1	2	3	4	

Without death, there would be no ticking of the clock and hence no time for gardening. We forget that the garden of midsummer emerged from the pure potentials of the bare soil in March and April. If the

1
3
5

	FRI.	SAT.	SUN.	MON.	TUES.
	5	6	7	8	9

garden stood eternally, we'd have no chance to grow another, to learn, and to create new varieties. This ruinous December weather reduces last summer's garden to potentials so that nature can rethink her last idea and state it again to see how it turns out, then learn a bit and restate it again, until the restatements lengthen into thousands, millions, and even billions of years of time. By constantly improving her idea each year, she has ended up with us. Obviously, the improvements are in little increments.

The garden's old age and death in this season also give us hope. Without death in this world, there could be no hope. We'd be here eternally, and that would be that. Hope is the belief that if we try to follow our inner lights, we'll participate in progress and things will get better. These are the questions that hopeful gardeners ask at the end of the year: How did my crops fare? Did I learn to cope with the bean beetle? Did I make mistakes? How can I do better next time? There's always a next time for a gardener. Beyond the deathly and frozen winter, the gardener knows that there's a warm sun waiting, and gentle rains, and the songs of birds. Gardeners are full of hope. Someday, when the gardener's own cycle draws to a close, such hope and knowledge will sustain him or her.

There are creative and destructive forces in the world, held in dynamic balance. In April, May, and June gardens, the creative forces are in ascendance. This is balanced by the garden in October, November, and December, when the destructive forces are most evident. The year, too, has its day and its night, as does the garden, as does the gardener.

But this is not the time of the night of the soul—far from it! The final days, because they are few, are sweeter. The tried-and-true recipe for enjoyment of life is to live every day as if it were your last. Sioux

WED.	THURS.	FRI.	SAT.	SUN.	
10	11	12	13	14	

braves rose to greet the day with this invocation: "Today is a fine day to die." The final taste of sweet, sweet life is savored the most.

But there goes the old year. It is finally reduced to nothing. The December darkness thickens and thickens until it becomes almost impossible to see. Let it go. The garden is only a memory now anyway. Heave one last sigh and close your eyes and dream of a place far away, with a garden bed ready for seeds, and a plum tree sprinkling its white flower petals on the bed, and a bird in the tree that sings the morning up.

⋙ The Perfect Gift ⋙

If you're a gardener, you probably have friends who are gardeners. Getting them a holiday present is always a challenge. But I have the answer. Give them the gift that has a thousand uses—all of them as yet undiscovered. Give them a dibble. Dibbles come with rustproof metal tang and hardwood handle and are guaranteed to last, mostly because they never get used. My dibble is still in the closet where I put it that Christmas Day many years ago. It's good as new. Dibbles are not for dabblers; they're a gift for serious gardeners. Serious gardeners need a good laugh.

1
3
7

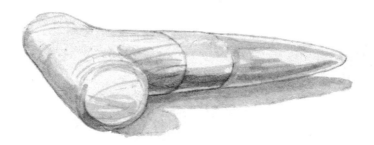

	MON.	TUES.	WED.	THURS.	FRI.
	15	16	17	18	19

138

SAT.	SUN.
20	21

Requiem

Under the wide and starry sky
  Dig the grave and let me lie:
Glad did I live and gladly die,
  And I laid me down with a will.

This be the verse you 'grave for me:
Here he lies where he long'd to be;
Home is the sailor, home from sea,
And the hunter home from the hill.

Robert Louis Stevenson

The New Natural Year: 1987

We leave the natural year of 1986 at 11:02 P.M. on Monday, December 22. At that point, the winter solstice occurs and the new natural year of 1987 is under way. The Period of Winter Solstice lasts until the new moon on Tuesday, December 30, 1986, at 10:10 P.M., when The Period of Lesser Cold begins. This lasts through New Year's Day and into 1987 itself.

Postscript

America made a great contribution to the world with its wilderness park system, but many of these are well-trammeled these days, and one has to go to far-distant places to find pristine wilderness.

It's my contention that people can contact this wilderness without traveling far from home. If we get small, if we kneel down and look into the garden, the weed patch, and the woods, we will soon see that nature still operates her immutable laws. Under the forsythia, down in the weeds, the predators stalk their prey, and nature is as red in tooth and claw as in the forest primeval. Even in our planted and manicured gardens, nature works her will. We presume too much when we feel nature can be chased from our neighborhoods by lawn mowers. The same processes that make for a wilderness make for the wild patch behind the shed. The blue jay may roost with equal ease in foundation plantings or in wilderness pine. The same soil bacteria decompose the duff on the wilderness floor as take our composts apart.

Just because man has had a hand in selecting plants and choosing sites doesn't mean that the result isn't natural and no longer answers to the call of the wild. If we abandon a yard or a forest for some years, we will see how loud that call still rings, even within city borders.

While wilderness areas are important reservoirs of wildness for large animals to live the Pleistocene life, they do not have a corner on nature or her laws. We can learn as much from the petunia as from the redwoods if we know how to look.

Appendixes

Holidays and Important Dates

December 1985
21 Winter solstice
25 Christmas Day

January 1986
1 New Year's Day
2 Earth at perihelion
6 Epiphany
15 Martin Luther King,
   Jr.'s birthday

February
2 Groundhog Day,
   Candlemas
9 Chinese New Year,
   4623 (Year of the Tiger)
10 Halley's Comet reaches
   perihelion
11 Shrove Tuesday
12 Ash Wednesday,
   Lincoln's birthday
14 Valentine's Day
15 Susan B. Anthony Day
16 First Sunday in Lent
17 Washington's birthday
   observed
22 Washington's birthday,
   traditional

March
17 St. Patrick's Day
20 Vernal equinox
23 Palm Sunday
28 Good Friday
30 Easter

April
1 April Fool's Day
13 Thomas Jefferson's
   birthday
24 First day of Passover
27 Daylight Saving Time
   begins
30 May Eve,
   Walpurgisnacht

May
1 May Day
11 Mother's Day
18 Pentecost, Whitsunday
21 Victoria Day (Canada)
26 Memorial Day observed
30 Memorial Day,
   traditional

June
13 Shavuot, Feast of
   Weeks
14 Flag Day
15 Father's Day
21 Summer solstice

July
1 Dominion Day (Canada)
4 Independence Day
5 Earth at aphelion
14 Bastille Day
31 August Eve, Lammas

1
4
2

September
1   Labor Day
23 Autumn equinox
28 American Indian Day

October
3   Jewish New Year, 5747
    (at sunset)
4   Rosh Hashanah
12 Columbus Day,
    traditional
13 Yom Kippur, Columbus
    Day observed
18 Succoth
24 United Nations Day
26 Standard Time begins
30 Mischief Night
31 Halloween

November
1   All Saint's Day
4   Election Day
11 Veteran's Day
17 Sadie Hawkins Day
27 Thanksgiving Day
30 First Sunday in Advent

December
7   Pearl Harbor Day
22 Winter solstice
25 Christmas Day
27 Hanukkah

∽ Planting by the Moon ∽

The simplest way to plant by the moon is to plant fruiting, flowering, and leafy crops when the moon is waxing; plant root crops when the moon is waning.

Periods of waxing moon in 1986:
January 11–25
February 9–23
March 11–25
April 10–23
May 9–22
June 8–21
July 8–20
August 6–18
September 5–17
October 4–16
November 3–15
December 2–15

Periods of waning moon in 1986:
January 27–February 7
February 25–March 9
March 26–April 8
April 24–May 7
May 24–June 6
June 23–July 6
July 22–August 4
August 20–September 3
September 19–October 2
October 18–November 1
November 17–30
December 17–30

Traditional Indian Names for the Full Moons

January: Wolf Moon
February: Snow Moon
March: Worm Moon or Crow Moon
April: Pink Moon
May: Flower Moon or Corn Planting Moon
June: Strawberry Moon
July: Buck Moon or Thunder Moon
August: Sturgeon Moon, Red Moon, or Green Corn Moon
September: Harvest Moon
October: Hunter's Moon
November: Beaver Moon
December: Cold Moon

Halley's Comet

If you don't have a telescope, December 1985 is the earliest you will be able to see the comet; it will become visible between Aquarius and Capricorn, low in the southern sky. In the evening sky, the comet will be visible from January 5 to January 25, 1986, and again from April 18 to April 25. It will be at its brightest while moving through the predawn sky on April 7. From February 26 to April 6, 1986, look for the comet in the sky before dawn. The comet's tail should be best developed between March 26 and April 6.

Astronomers are not expecting Halley's to be anywhere near as bright and spectacular as accounts from past apparitions might lead us to expect. In fact, the earth will simply be in the wrong position relative to the comet and the sun to give us the best view. Observation of Halley's this time around will be better for people viewing from the Southern Hemisphere. The farther south we go, the higher the comet will appear in the sky. But although the comet will be low in the southern sky for us in the Northern Hemisphere, it will still be as bright. Observing Halley's Comet will still be a once-in-a-lifetime experience for most of us. It won't be back for 75 years.

Derrick H. Pitts

Major Meteor Showers in 1986

Peak Date	Name	Number per Hour	Moon Phase
Jan. 4	Quadrantids	40	last quarter
Apr. 22	Lyrids	15	full moon
May 4	Aquarids	20	last quarter
July 28	Aquarids	20	last quarter
Aug. 12	Perseids	50	first quarter
Oct. 21	Orionids	25	full moon
Nov. 3	Taurids	15	new moon
Nov. 17	Leonids	15	full moon
Dec. 14	Geminids	50	full moon
Dec. 22	Ursids	15	last quarter

Eclipses in 1986

April 9: Partial solar eclipse
April 24: Total lunar eclipse
October 3: Total solar eclipse visible in the North Atlantic
October 17: Total lunar eclipse

∾ Visible Planets for 1986 ∾

January 15: Venus moves from Scorpio into Sagittarius. Mars is in Virgo. Jupiter is in Capricorn. Saturn moves from Libra into Scorpio.

February 15: Venus moves from Aquarius into Pisces. Mars moves from Virgo into Libra. Jupiter is in Capricorn. Saturn is in Scorpio, where it remains for the rest of the year.

March 15: Venus moves from Pisces into Aries. Mars is in Libra. Jupiter moves into Aquarius.

April 15: Venus moves through Taurus into Gemini. Mars moves from Libra into Scorpio. Jupiter settles into Aquarius for the rest of the year.

May 15: Venus is in Cancer. Mars joins Saturn in Scorpio.

June 15: Venus moves into Leo. Mars moves from Scorpio into Sagittarius.

July 15: Venus moves through Virgo into Libra and Mars holds a position in Sagittarius.

August 15: Venus moves through Scorpio into Sagittarius. Mars moves into Capricorn.

September 15: Venus is in Capricorn all month, along with Mars.

October 15: Venus moves through Aquarius into Pisces. Mars teams up with Jupiter in Aquarius.

November 15: Venus moves through Aries into Taurus while Mars moves from Pisces into Aries.

December 15: The year's end finds Venus in Gemini, Mars in Aries, Jupiter in Aquarius, and Saturn in Scorpio.

Bright Stars in 1986

Winter Sky: Aldebaran in Taurus; Rigel, Bellatrix, Betelgeuse, Saiph in Orion; Sirius in Canis Major; Procyon in Canis Minor; Capella in Auriga; Algol in Perseus.

Spring Sky: Regulus in Leo; Castor and Pollux in Gemini.

Summer Sky: Altair in Aquila; Deneb in Cygnus; Spica in Virgo; Arcturus in Bootes; Fomalhaut in Pisces Austrinus.

Autumn Sky: Algol in Perseus; Antares in Scorpio.

Frost-Free Growing Seasons

City	Mean Date for Last 32° Day in Spring	Mean Freeze-Free Period (in days)	Mean Date for First 32° Day in Fall
Albuquerque, NM	Apr. 16	196	Oct. 29
Allentown, PA	Apr. 14	192	Oct. 23
Anchorage, AK	May 17	130	Sept. 18
Annapolis, MD	Mar. 30	234	Nov. 15
Atlanta, GA	Mar. 1	242	Nov. 18
Billings, MT	May 15	132	Sept. 24
Birmingham, AL	Mar. 19	241	Nov. 14
Bismarck, ND	May 11	136	Sept. 24
Boise, ID	May 6	159	Oct. 12
Boston, MA	Apr. 16	192	Oct. 25
Burlington, VT	May 8	148	Oct. 3
Charleston, WV	Apr. 18	193	Oct. 28
Charlotte, NC	Mar. 21	239	Nov. 15
Cheyenne, WY	May 20	130	Sept. 27
Chicago, IL	Apr. 19	192	Oct. 28
Cincinnati, OH	Apr. 15	192	Oct. 25
Concord, NH	May 11	142	Sept. 30
Denver, CO	May 3	166	Oct. 16
Des Moines, IA	Apr. 19	186	Oct. 22
Detroit, MI	Apr. 4	181	Oct. 22
Greenville, SC	Mar. 23	239	Nov. 17
Hartford, CT	Apr. 22	180	Oct. 19
Houston, TX	Feb. 4	309	Dec. 10
Indianapolis, IN	Apr. 17	193	Oct. 27
Jackson, MS	Mar. 10	248	Nov. 13
Jacksonville, FL	Feb. 6	313	Dec. 16
Kansas City, MO	Apr. 6	207	Oct. 30

City	Mean Date for Last 32° Day in Spring	Mean Freeze-Free Period (in days)	Mean Date for First 32° Day in Fall
Las Vegas, NV	Mar. 13	245	Nov. 13
Lexington, KY	Apr. 13	198	Oct. 28
Lincoln, NE	Apr. 20	180	Oct. 17
Little Rock, AR	Mar. 17	238	Nov. 10
Madison, WI	Apr. 26	177	Oct. 19
Memphis, TN	Mar. 20	237	Nov. 12
Minneapolis, MN	Apr. 30	166	Oct. 13
New Orleans, LA	Feb. 13	302	Dec. 12
New York, NY	Apr. 7	219	Nov. 12
Norfolk, VA	Mar. 5	244	Nov. 2
Oklahoma City, OK	Mar. 28	223	Nov. 7
Phoenix, AZ	Jan. 28	322	Dec. 16
Portland, ME	Apr. 15	161	Sept. 23
Portland, OR	Feb. 25	279	Dec. 1
Providence, RI	Apr. 13	197	Oct. 27
Salt Lake City, UT	Apr. 12	202	Nov. 1
San Francisco, CA	frost less than 1 year in 10		
Seattle, WA	Feb. 23	280	Nov. 30
Sioux Falls, SD	May 5	152	Oct. 3
Topeka, KS	Apr. 9	200	Oct. 26
Trenton, NJ	Apr. 4	218	Nov. 8
Washington, DC	Mar. 29	225	Nov. 9
Wilmington, DE	Apr. 18	191	Oct. 26

SOURCE: Officials of the National Oceanic and Atmospheric Administration, U.S. Department of Commerce, *Climates of the States*, vol. 1 and 2 (Port Washington, N.Y.: Water Information Center, 1974).

Weeds as Indicators of Soil Type

The weeds that grow on your property can give clues to what your soil is like. Following is a listing of some weeds that grow in particular types of soils.

Rich, fertile soil:
chickweed
common groundsel
lamb's-quarters
ragweed

Poor soil:
mugwort
mullein
wild carrot
wild parsnip

Light, sandy soil:
aster
cornflower
field horsetail
ragweed
white clover
wild lettuce

Heavy, clay soil:
annual sow-thistle
Canada thistle
creeping buttercup
dandelion
English daisy
quackgrass

Moist soil:
cotton grass
false hellebore
garden sorrel
hedge bindweed
marsh horsetail
mosses
narrow-leaved goldenrod
rushes
sedges

Dry soil:
leafy spurge
prostrate pigweed
Russian thistle
silvery cinquefoil
wild mustard

Acid soil:
daisy
horsetails
knapweeds
nettles
wild radish
wild strawberry

Alkaline soil:
blue cornflower
creeping bellflower
spurry
white mustard

❧ Companion Plants ❧

Here's a list of traditional garden companions. They may or may not work for you, but many gardeners swear by them.

Asparagus: basil, parsley, pot marigold, tomatoes

Beans: cabbage family, carrots, celery, corn, cucumbers, eggplant, marigold, nasturtium, peas, potatoes, radishes, Swiss chard

Beets: bush beans, cabbage family, garlic, lettuce, onions

Cabbage Family: beets, celery, cucumbers, dill, garlic, lettuce, mint, nasturtium, onions, potatoes, spinach, rosemary

Carrots: beans, lettuce, onions, peas, peppers, radishes, rosemary, sage, tomatoes

Celery: beans, cabbage family, chives, garlic, nasturtium, squash, tomatoes

Corn: beans, cucumbers, melons, odorless marigold, parsley, peas, potatoes, pumpkins, squash

Cucumbers: beans, cabbage family, corn, oregano, peas, radishes, tomatoes

Eggplant: beans, peppers

Lettuce: beets, cabbage family, carrots, chives, garlic, onions, radishes

Parsley: asparagus, corn, tomatoes

Peas: beans, carrots, chives, corn, cucumbers, radishes, turnips

Peppers: carrots, eggplant, onions, tomatoes

Potatoes: beans, cabbage family, corn, eggplant, horseradish, peas

Pumpkins: corn, melons, oregano, squash

Radishes: beans, carrots, cucumbers, lettuce, melons, peas

Spinach: cabbage family, oregano, strawberry, nasturtium

Squash: corn, melons, nasturtium, oregano, pumpkins

Swiss Chard: beans, cabbage family, onions

Tomatoes: asparagus, basil, carrots, celery, chives, cucumber, dill, onion, parsley, marigolds, peppers

Turnips: peas

World Records

Following is a selected listing of fruits and vegetables holding world records for the biggest of their kind as of 1984. Information comes from the *Guinness Book of World Records* (New York: Sterling Publishing Co., 1984).

Broccoli	28 lb., 14¾ oz.	West Sussex, England, 1964
Red cabbage	123 lb.	County Durham, England, 1865
Cantaloupe	55 lb.	Rocky Mountain, N.C., 1983
Carrot	15 lb., 7 oz.	Nelson, New Zealand, 1978
Cauliflower	52 lb., 11½ oz.	West Sussex, England, 1966
Celery	35 lb.	Merseyside, England, 1973
Cucumber (length)	38.37 in.	Knott, Texas, 1983
Gourd (weight)	196 lb.	Suffolk, England, 1846
Gourd (length)	82 in.	Poland, Ohio, 1977
Lemon	8 lb., 8 oz.	Whittier, California, 1983
Lettuce	25 lb.	Merseyside, England, 1974
Orange	5 lb., 8 oz.	Nelspruit, South Africa, 1981
Potato	161 lb.	Chester, England, 1795
Pumpkin	493 lb., 8 oz.	Nova Scotia, 1983
Radish	25 lb.	Ruskin, Florida, 1977
Squash	513 lb.	Ninevah, Indiana, 1977
Strawberry	7¼ oz.	Essex, England, 1977
Tomato	6 lb., 8 oz.	Monona, Wisconsin, 1977
Turnip	73 lb.	1768 (origin unlisted)
Watermelon	255 lb.	Bixby, Oklahoma, 1983

Traditional Weather Indicators

Expect good weather when:
The clouds are high — the higher the clouds, the better the
    weather.
The wind is still.
The wind is in the west.
The sky is red at sunset.
Cirrus clouds dissolve and seem to vanish.
Cumulus clouds are smaller at sunset than they were at
    noon.
The full moon rises clear.
Fog rises, or comes from seaward.
The dew is on the grass.
Cats wash themselves.
Birds fly high.
Ants scatter.

Bad weather is on the way when:
The sky is gray at sunset and red at sunrise.
There are yellow streaks in the sunset sky.
Smoke does not rise.
Clouds fly against the wind.
Fog settles, or comes from landward.
Stars appear to twinkle more than normal.
The moon has a halo — the larger the halo, the sooner the
    rain will come.
Ropes and guitar strings shorten.
Trees show the undersides of their leaves.
The scent of flowers is unusually noticeable.
Corns and bunions throb; joints ache.
Cows huddle at one end of the field and turn their tails to
    the wind.
Bees stay close to the hive.
Cats lick their coats against the grain.
Ants travel in lines.

Some long-range weather indicators:
If there is no snow before January there will be more in
    March and April.

(continued)

A warm January brings a cold May.

There is always one fine week in February.

As it rains in March, so it rains in June.

A moist April means a clear June.

A dry May is followed by a wet June.

A wet May portends a dry July.

Whatever July and August boil, September cannot fry.

Heavy rains bring drought.

Much rain in October foretells much wind in December.

If it's warm in October, it will be cold in February.

A late spring is a great blessing.

If spring is cold and wet, autumn will be cold and dry.

A dry spring is followed by a rainy summer.

A moist and cool summer portends a hard winter.

There can never be too much rain before midsummer.

A late spring is good for corn but bad for cattle.

After a rainy winter follows a fruitful spring.

A wet year is followed by a cold one.

Wet and dry years come in triads.

SOURCE: Edward B. Garriot, *Weather Folk-Lore and Local Weather Signs* (Washington, D.C.: United States Department of Agriculture, 1903).